Old Coder Guy Book 1

Absurdity and Dubious Wisdom from an Accidental 30 Year Career in Technology

By Eric Whitney

Published by OCG Worldwide LLC

(Whoever had "the company OCG made up in satire videos is now real, and has published a fucking book", congratulations, you're a winner!)

ISBN: 979-8-9882697-0-0

First Printing, 2023

CONTENTS |

Introduction

I'm going to be honest, at one point I seriously thought about writing this entire book as a two-person dialog between me and you, and to facilitate that, I was going to leave blanks throughout the book where, before you started reading, you'd write your name in, something like three or four hundred times. There was going to be a special edition for C-suite readers that came with a crayon, so you could pick up a copy at an airport bookstore or complementary at a Centurion lounge and fill your name in sitting in business class while you were waiting on Patricia to freshen your departure champagne.

"Rick", writes Rick, pressing just hard enough not to break the crayon. Rick smiles to himself. It's nice to see his own name right there in the book.

Page 2. "Rick", "Rick", "Rick". So satisfying.

Feeling like a collaborator and an author, Rick raises his nearly empty champagne glass and shakes it slightly toward a flight attendant, not Tricia, clearly supporting a different part of business class.

Page 3. "Rick", and a little later "Rick". It's hard to keep the crayon from hitting the text above and below, but "fuck it, this is my book", murmurs Rick. Rick stretches his legs and curls his toes as Trish brings him a fresh, cool glass. It's good to be Rick.

And then my wife said, "but the audiobook will sound like you're having a seven-hour stroke", and here we are, no personalization, no crayon, no giggles of delight.

This is a weird book.

What This Book Is

It is a mix of true stories that sound like fiction and my real learnings and advice, served under a pint of absurdity, profanity, and silliness gravy. As such, I recommend both that you not take it too seriously and be careful how you use it.

However, you *should* use this book as a formal quoted reference in academic or professional settings absolutely every chance you get. I'm going to do my best to make sure that any highly quotable lightning-bolt genius level insights which by some accident end up in this book, are well decorated with salty language. Remember: any time an uncensored OCG quote appears in a term paper, a business presentation or ideally on a Ted talk screen, the Doomsday Clock glitch-pauses for a whole Texas second (~1.3954 Unix seconds).

In the comment threads, some people have referred to Old Coder Guy's *cynicism*. I can understand how that could be an interpretation of a steady stream of videos where things are going so wrong for our main characters. But let me say clearly: I don't intend for OCG to be cynical, and I feel like it's the wrong word.

The first line of Tolstoy's Anna Karenina has always stuck in my mind. "Happy families are all alike; every unhappy family is unhappy in its own way." Happiness is great, but its homogeny makes it somewhat uninteresting. Other people's beach photos... meh. Other people's time-we-lived-at-a-landfill-for-a-week-with-no-supplies videos... yes, please.

But further, unhappiness (with its cousins mistake, failure, bad luck) is where all learning happens.

This book will range schizophrenically between topics, like ordering a Denny's full breakfast and getting plates with pancakes, a whole uncut watermelon, and a boot full of chicken noodle soup. The only cohesion problems here are your expectations. If it helps, you can find the narrative spine through the truth that all of this happened in and to one human life and one human mind.

I know a lot of people who have found success, satisfaction, and happiness in their tech or management career, sometimes. If you're interested in that particular lens, spend more time on that steaming pile LinkedIn.

But on OCG, and here in this book, we're going to mostly talk about how things go sideways. I'm going to wait until at least my third book before I start an argument with that fucker Tolstoy.

Given all of these caveats and qualifications, you might ask, "well then, who is this book *for*?". Before we flush ourselves down that pipe, let us address the topic of profanity. Simply put, there will be an abundance.

Profanity

If we think of comedy and profane language as similar to spice levels in curry, for this book, I'm shooting for medium... like .5 Chappelles or .8 Bill Burrs. My line is drawn around a moderate use of F bombs, a substantial serving of shits, hells, damns, with some light potty references. You certainly won't see many ****s, ****s, or **********s.

The role of profanity in the OCG universe is to help calibrate the voice and tone to a Friday happy hour at the pub with a few close friends-from-work. These are the unfiltered stories from our days spent behind our humming plastic boxes prostituting our mind-capacity, told without needing to bite your tongue to keep from saying the thing that could tank your career.

It's interesting to me that while the professional world is gushing over ChatGPT and generative AI as potential work-optimizers, we gladly accept and operate with a highly inefficient work-muzzle that keeps the truth from plainly surfacing and circulating in all our professional environments. These protocols are like a cage hoop skirt over our true thoughts, but instead of ensuring that no one knows if *you have* a big ass, they prevent people who work with you from knowing that *they might be* a big ass. Along with probably 50%+ of the problems, failures, incompetencies, and frictions, which are collectively the reasons why you didn't ship in Q4 and why your site and app are so slow and awful.

OK, I reread that, and on second look, I can see hints of a few potential concerns with all of us bringing our totally unfiltered true selves to the office. Yes, *especially* you.

Maybe the closest analogy is the increasingly ubiquitous "bring your dog to work" policy. I feel like the original COO who signed off on this must have either been an unsavable dog addict, or someone who had only ever seen dogs on calendars and in Grated movies, and didn't realize that, taken in whole, dogs are mischievous savage killers.

I have a friend that breeds and trains Belgian Malinois. His original male, Shadow, is one of the most terrifying beings I've ever met. He's getting a bit codgery now, but at age two or three, when Shadow got bored, he would take furniture irreparably apart. I don't mean tear up a pillow, I mean reduce an entire couch to its molecular components. More than once, and I'm not making this up, he pulled sheets of drywall off the walls. Imagine you leave a dog for an hour in a dining room and come back to a significantly progressing open floor plan construction site.

If you're sitting in an open-floor-plan developer factory farm and Angela the basset hound waddles by, you might turn away from your mandatory learning module due in about 31 minutes, educating you that email from rnicrosoft.com is probably a phishing attack, and watch Angela for a moment. You may even issue two pumps of closed-mouth chuckle, mhum, mhum, and get a nice micro dose of dopamine that enables you to turn back to your machine and resume letting it shave off your soul like a cheese grater for three more hours.

But if that dog was Shadow, and he turned down your row, stopped at you, and you realized you may smell like weed because you dropped by your mom's house before work, your bowels would likely release. Having Paco the psychopathic chihuahua or Lord Diddy the terrier, bark-whip you every time you go to the bathroom or kitchen would have even Steve Irwin reaching for the bacon-wrapped arsenic.

A dogs-at-work policy, regardless of what your unhinged dog-parent COO might argue, isn't *all dogs no matter what*. It presumes an ability for the dog to keep its shit together and still *be a dog but be a dog that can coexist* with a safe, sane, and productive work environment.

Similarly, creating a profanity-safe work environment is no doubt challenging. In fact, so much so that I would never recommend it. But a profanity-safe work happy hour among a small group of trusted same-level colleagues is a yes, absolutely. Like this book.

Use Cases for this Book by User Persona

If you're a **librarian**, this book is most certainly for you. There is going to be a good amount of fuckery and controversial professional advice, to a degree that we could probably pass a should-ban-it test in the American states that border a gulf or have no access to ocean. "But why would I want more of that, I already have to lie to my doctor about my drinking?" you might ask.

By example, let's consider a passenger-capable hot air balloon. When the balloon starts out, it has a bunch of zero-value heavy shit, like bags of sand, tied to it to help it stay down. The sand isn't going on the trip, however, its sole function being to be available to be jettisoned so the balloon can fly higher.

For your library, this book is your bag of sand. You need us so when the banning-burning dipshits show up, like the book version of the Secret Service, we'll take a slug to the chest so that other books might continue to serve our country. Make sure we're on the display table just inside the door with a sign that says "Fuckery Nonfiction", and we'll take it from there. I'm not drawing a map for people angry at words, but this is a debt I owe to books I won't list, which I'm glad to pay in number-of-mentions in schoolboard minutes, and maybe a few heroic ultimate-sacrifice copies lost to unfortunate but honorable parking-lot-barrel Viking funerals. I'm glad to do my part to take some of the heat off the ones that matter.

I'm going to say this again because I anticipate confusion. For librarians, this book is your honeypot, with nothing of value, meant to be a no-downside sacrifice so you can appease the torch-and-pitchfork crew. This is like those inflatable fake tanks the allies used in dubya dubya two to keep the real, critical equipment and personnel from getting attacked. We're the book equivalent of the old guy saying "go on, save yourselves, I've lived a full life… I'll stay here with two bullets left in my .38 and show these zombies I don't taste like chicken".

And if you're in a pinch where you feel only a traditional book burning will satisfy the rabble, you are fully green-lit for that by me, the author. But please… please. Find a drag queen to do it.

If you're a **student** who picked this book up at the library from the table described above, you've likely confused "fuckery", which is used here as a business and technology term, with "pornography", which you can find in the bottom drawer of the librarian's desk under the scotch and the revolver.

If you found this book under other circumstances, such as a **bookstore** shelf or browsing an online retailer, the chances are good that if you've gotten this far, you already own it. Since you're committed, I suggest you see it through but start composing a savage review in your mind in case the rest of it goes, based on what you've read so far, about how it seems it will.

If you received this book as a **gift**, then you, my friend, are truly loved. Your gifter is someone who saw this book, knows your brain, and thought "this software will run great on that hardware". Yes, for some readers, that may be perceived as an insult, and may make you want to fight your gifter. If your gifter is that fuck Kyle, we're on the same page. But for the rest of you, you should take this as a great complement regarding your standing with your gift-giving friend, colleague, or family member.

Unless your friend just bought copies to give out to seem Gucci but hasn't read the book yet. That's a friend that would surprise you with Ayahuasca in your Monday morning coffee before sprint planning, just so someone else was doing it with them. If you track friendships correctly, and by that I mean in a swimlane diagram, you need to move this one into the "Not even at Burning Man" lane.

And finally, you may be here because you found my satire and "advice" **videos** and thought "sure, I'd read a book that was something like that". If this is you, and you choose to continue forward and read the book, please connect with me immediately on a social platform and set our relationship to "It's Complicated". It's time to set some ground rules and expectations.

Books... I'll write this slowly... are *different* than videos.

One easy test you can run right now is to just look at these words, but make your eyes stop moving. If you're still reading this, you're not doing it right. Don't keep moving your eyes, just stare at this word and don't keep going.

If this were a video, this shit would still be moving around, even if your head and eyes were totally still. But with a book, if your eyes stop moving, the words just sit there and nothing happens. I hope this simple demonstration makes this key difference between videos and books clear for you. If you're still looking at the same words from earlier, you can stop the test now, and go back to moving your eyes so you can catch back up and we can move on.

Another way books generally, and this book specifically, are different than my videos is that books are usually longer. A video runs a minute, maybe five at the max, but if you got a three-minute-long book, you'd be waving it around getting kind of pissed, and it would flop a lot because it's really more of a pamphlet at that point. "You ain't Lao Tzu motherfucker, I paid for some pages", is something you might say, before taking a long emphasis-suck from a tube or box that combines some kind of smoke or mist with earth air.

So, to emphasize, if you've watched my videos, welcome... but please adapt your expectations.

if (this ==== true)

Every story about people and events in this book is 100% true. Given that the OCG videos dabble in the fantastic and hyperbolic, I can understand why you might find some of these tales exagerated. They are not.

Vis-à-vis Dipshits and Fucks

And finally, as you're reading, one question that will likely occur to you is "am *I* one of the so-called dipshits or fucks he's referring to here?"

In the unparalled 1992 tech-western, *Unforgiven*, this exact question is addressed near the climax, in the following exchange between n00b technologist "the Kid", and William "Punchcard" Munny, a grizzled and recently involuntarily un-retired CTO, played by Clint Eastwood.

"Yeah, well, I guess they had it coming", says the Kid, overcome with regret after his first time referring to another technologist as a dipshit.

The Kid takes a long, sorrowful chug from a whiskey bottle usually reserved for sprint planning. The camera cuts to Clint, whose face shows the gray and wear from decades of calling-out thousands of dipshits and fucks.

"We all have it coming, kid."

OK, people, it's game time. Hands in the middle.

"Let's read this fucking book!" on three.

One... two...

21

People

I Am Not That Smart

Before we talk about other people, I think it's probably a good idea to turn the microscope inward and make some statements about myself.

If you're here because you've watched the OCG videos, this may surprise you, but there are several things I don't know.

We'll talk about this more in a later chapter where I go through my creative process, but for now the key point is that you've likely been misled by my OCG-favorable topic selection and editing skills into believing I walk around like the fucking Delphic Oracle, an expert on every subject and its future trajectory.

What is more true is that on most topics, I'm guy-who-runs-with-scissors. I usually have some B/B- ideas, but I might go to war for something I realize later was D+ on its best day. That really nullifies any value from the B ideas because I passionately sell high and low quality with no distinction, so you can't really trust any of it.

As such, I suggest you look at the views expressed in this book, not as any kind of career or life guidebook, but instead as "one way to think about it", coming from a highly subjective and near steamroller-grade single opinion. When I say, "you should do this thing", I really mean "as you decide what to do, you may want to consider this alongside all of the other quackery and mumbo jumbo".

Or, you can replace all of your current Policy, Training, and Best Practices documentation with this book, starting Monday. Like most of your critical decisions, it should probably be left up to a coin flip or a game of rock paper scissors with your leadership team.

But regardless of your adoption path related to *what I say* in this book, I think you could certainly benefit from considering *how I say it*. And by that I mean that you should try to apply the word "fuck" to your point of view about more things in your life.

A machine can *have* a point of view, but **you** can *care* about your point of view. Every minute you spend on something that you can't describe in some way using the word "fuck" is probably precious lifetime you're wasting on something that doesn't matter to you enough.

The "fuck lens" can be bad or good. It can help you identify the things you need to do more of and the people you need to see more of, and those of both categories that you need to try to get away from.

A "huge fucking problem" is likely a worthy foe, but a standard "problem" may not be.

A person who makes you feel fucking alive and tells stories that leave you fucking dead or fucking crying, is probably somebody to hang on to.

A fucking job, a fucking company, a fucking boss, should probably go into your only-for-now list.

To be clear, your "fuck" word doesn't need to be "fuck", or even, by societal standards, profane. Just search your vocabulary for how you describe exceptionally great or exceptionally awful situations, and those are *your* words.

I'm fucking pumped to be writing this book and fucking power-hip-thrust super-stoked that you're reading it.

Also, safety tip, definitely don't Google "fuck word" on your office network. But "fuck lens" is safe to search at work, it will bring up some great Harvard Business Review articles about collaboration, you should take a look.

Yes, We Know How To "Technology", So What

Taking a step back for a minute, can you imagine how fucked up everyone's hair was in ten or twenty thousand BC, before they figured out how to work with metal?

Of course, some Mesolithic-obsessed reader just yelled out "obsidian knife", but not everyone lived near a volcano, *Kyle*. If your people started near an active volcano, and they weren't stuck on an island with nowhere to run, your tribe likely spent the next thousand years trying to get as far away from that bullshit as possible. I mean, molten fucking rock shooting out of the ground. Year 10,000 BC you see shit like that and you're not waiting around for an insurance check... it's time to pack up the elders and GTFO.

Grok: "Hole in ground smoke again."

Thak: "Ground angry we not throw Colleen in yet."

Colleen: "The fuck you say?"

Grok: "Thak right. Ground like ladies. Throw in Colleen, ground happy, stay here."

Colleen: "How did you two dipshits skip over all the other options to 'ground like ladies'? If the ground wants something, maybe it's a magazine or a chicken sandwich. Maybe the ground is into *dudes*."

Grok and Thak nervously exchange glances. Grok: "Ground not like dudes… ground like ladies."

Colleen: "Or… we could just pick up our valuable shit, which is pretty much my pelt bed, those two clam shells, and the good stick, and move the fuck somewhere else where the ground is chill."

Thak, relieved: "Colleen wise", but then misreads the moment and proceeds to segue into a confusing marriage proposal by bludgeoning Grok to death with a rock.

But let's address this "obsidian knife" point. Sure, compared to alternatives, which we'll discuss below, a sharp edge is preferred. However, if you think you're going to get a stone knife haircut and not look like a fucking lunatic, I'd like to challenge you to cut your own hair with a steak knife and go to work tomorrow. This is one of those cases where I confidently feel like I don't need a crystal ball, but if one of you point-provers wants to die on the "bet I can give myself a nice haircut with a steak knife" hill, please send me a photo.

Absent the sharp rock, though, plans B and C take a hard turn off the pavement and into the swamp. Imagine your thick matted self finally making the tough call and seeking out the local surgeon slash barber slash what-do-those-lights-in-the-sky-mean guy. The tools of the day were likely either a rounded chunk of granite or actual fucking fire. That's not at all meant to be cool children's slang, I mean literal hot burning fire. I've probably watched 50 videos of people jumping off roofs into swimming pools, but I haven't seen a damn soul with the bits (and honestly, willingness to honor their long-ago ancestors) to post a video of them beating their hair off with a rock or using a traditional cave torch to singe their unruly mop down to church-length.

So, it's 8,000 B.C., and you're walking around trying to be cool with your new do, which is a shell-like singed helmet, thinking to yourself "that tech bro putting curved edges on that rock is the fucking future, Ima blow the conch at him and make moves".

My point here is that...

To any far-future observers, we're all a bunch of backward-assed primitive twits.

Ten years from now, your best technology will trigger nostalgia. "Remember when we'd get those flip video cameras and take *digital* video when we were out doing stuff and then copy it to our computer, and it was so much easier than video tape? *And then smart phones happened?*"

Twenty years from now, it will embarrass you to talk about your current primary programming language, in which you invested thousands of hours, and which, at that future time, will be 2,000% less impressive than being able to start a fire by rubbing two sticks together.

Fifty years from now, talking about your technology from today, all of it in every context, will make you seem like those bowler hat and double-breasted-suit wearing 1900 New York City Bowery peasants, photographed as they see a camera for the first time with a look on their faces like they just met a centaur named Ding Dong.

It goes without saying that being alive in 8,000 B.C. was simpler, easier, and preferable in every way, but to highlight just one reason, the pace of innovation was snail divided by a million. The legend that some dude was working on a "rounded rock that would change transportation forever" was passed down for like fourteen generations before that shit rolled by. Startup founders' great-great-grandchildren were *still* in stealth.

But now things change quickly. I hope people take a moment to appreciate this: there have only been a relatively few generations in all of human history where the knowledge and expertise of a parent era has so little direct relevance and value in the lifetime of the children as is the case now. This is a simple and amazing mental exercise: consider what you understand about your ancestors living 30, 60, and 90 years ago.

35 years ago, I had effectively never used a computer. The most technological component in my life was a four-track analog cassette tape recorder. And that made me rural Ohio Elon Fucking Musk.

The best we are is experts *for now*. And in the technology context, "now" is a shockingly short span of time.

"In practical terms, what am I to do with this perspective?" might be something you're currently thinking.

Firstly, I recommend recalibrating your how-it-should-be-done technical discussion persona down from "maximum snark" to "the best idea in the room will be diaper-grade in twenty years, and by that standard, the only difference between your idea and my idea is that your baby had too much fiber".

This has also affected my view of the appropriate depth of learning for any technology. Yes, there will be situations where your solution is operating at the edge of the relevant scale, cost, and performance considerations, and developing a deep understanding of how the associated technologies work is critical. But for most systems there's a good-enough level, and rather than learning slightly better methods in one language or tool, you'd gain more value from a learning investment in other components of the system. For example, if you're an app-tier person, understanding the front end or the database will probably yield more benefits for both you and the project than learning more obscure Python, C#, or Java functions or patterns that let you do what you're already doing with a few less lines of code.

The process I've adopted for a few years is to learn the basics in a new tool or language, use it to do work, and only go deeper if I hit a clear tangible limitation. The side effect of this is that it keeps your code simple and agnostic, in the sense that you won't be incorporating... I don't want to say "syntactic sugar" because it's my version of the "moist aversion" and the words trigger me, but, well, that.

I think the guitar (yes, the instrument) is a great analogy. Despite the simplicity of the six-string basic structure, the range of techniques that can be applied to, and the sounds that can be coaxed or tortured from, a guitar, may be unique throughout music. From basic blues, the seemingly unlimited three and four chord songs from pop, folk, rock and country, to virtuosos from Hendrix to Stanley Jordan to Van Halen to Prince to Vai to these guys from Polyphia, the list goes on and on, there are thousands of very different answers to the question "how far can we push this". And because this is creative expression and entertainment, I say "fantastic... blow our minds".

Programming could be the same thing, but much more extreme. There are way more than six (or 7 or 8) strings and 22 (or 24) frets. Even the most limited programming language is like a guitar that is also a theremin, bagpipes and a fucking didgeridoo.

But other than for comedy purposes, the last thing the world needs is anyone using a programming language as a means of self-expression that tests the boundaries of imagination and inscrutability. If I get a codebase to maintain that looks like three hours of amphetamine-fueled Thelonious Monk "Round Midnight" explorations, I'm not likely to respond with "cool".

In summary, at our best, we are only the best *for now*, so check that ego. And please do the rest of us a favor and stick with A, D, E, in any order.

The Confidence Continuum

At the very beginning, you don't know what you're doing, and you know you don't know what you're doing.

And then there will be one type of work that you do more, and one tool or language that you use more, and you'll figure out some legitimately confusing stuff, and start to feel like you *understand*. At that point you become one of two kinds of people.

The first are the people who can never believe in themselves. They always feel like the one imposter hiding in plain sight among experts, waiting to be found out and kicked to the curb like the dipshits they believe themselves to be. And then they get some positive recognition, which only makes them feel worse, because it underscores how much they've fooled their managers into believing them to be anything other than incompetent fucks.

This happens a lot in tech. If this sounds like you, try to hear these words: I have never met a single person who thought and felt this way *who was right*. Not a single fucking one. Further, this belief system is a Möbius loop... it takes a lot of knowledge to be qualified to accurately judge your own incompetence.

You may not be the Kelly fucking Clarkson of C# or JavaScript or whatever the fuck they pay you to do, but I can promise you, if no one has ever brought you into a closed-door one-on-one to discuss your shitty performance, you're at least "good". And you may actually be the Kelly goddamn Clarkson of your domain... it's hard for me to say for certain based on our limited interactions. But I can absolutely fucking promise you that *you do not suck*. I know this can be hard if you're not wired this way but do your best to get past this way of thinking. It inhibits you, and life is too fucking short. Save your judgmental personal retrospective for your deathbed like the rest of us, and in the meantime, get out there and snap necks and cash checks like the boss bitch you were born to be.

The second group are the fucks that reach the understanding phase and have no qualms about believing in themselves. Just like group one, these dipshits are wrong almost every day.

One thing about programming that's kind of unique, is that the totality of your immersion into whatever *you* are working on has a way of shutting out your recognition of how many *other people* are simultaneously doing cool things with technology. I realize this is a giant subjective leap, but think about it for a few minutes and if you believe I'm wrong, which means you believe you're constantly considering all of the people moving and manipulating data, writing cool apps and web sites, making fast, interesting APIs, while deeply understanding 10 or 20 different languages, frameworks, and base design patterns, then you should skip this section because you are fucking perfect.

OK, so at least now we're being honest with ourselves.

To do tech work with high confidence is to some degree to wear blinders related to how insignificant what you're doing is related to the totality of work going on in our domain. It's a bit like someone who writes a couple of really punchy emails and thinks that they're somehow the Maya Angelou of corporate status updates, and not just one of the approximately hundred-million average dipshits who managed to get they're, their and there right again today.

The overconfidence of a confident tech worker is astounding. You could get whiplash watching them sprint past on their way to judge approaches, tools and languages they don't understand as well as they think they do.

The longer I live the more I appreciate and try to embrace a perpetual-student mindset.

The line representing the precisely appropriate level of confidence in your tech knowledge is one atom wide. Everything to the left is tragic pessimism, while everything to the right is baseless hollow bravado. In the history of programming there have been no more than three people who were able to sustain a perch exactly on that summit, and two of those heroes worked on, believe it or not, Healthcare.gov.

Do your best to find that summit and stand on that line, but in the meantime try to be neither the dipshit who knows they're right, or the Eeyore who's certain they aren't.

The Lessons of Don Boscoe

I met Don Boscoe when I interviewed him for a job in 2006. I don't remember that at all, he clearly made almost no impression at that time, which in hindsight is a somewhat troubling indicator of my potentially broken threat radar.

He was the referral of one of the earliest employees I hired for a tech services startup, and that guy was great, so I asked him if he had anyone he would recommend, and he offered two people, one of whom was Don Boscoe.

While we certainly must have met a couple of times earlier, including that interview, my earliest memory of Don Boscoe is still crystal clear in my mind.

Our startup was small but growing quickly due to a large contract with a Fortune 500 customer, who we'll refer to here as

The Client. This was before remote work, and we had a small office in a small town just north of Columbus Ohio. We had been hiring quickly, going from five people in August of 2005, to 20 or so in early 2006. Office space was constantly a struggle, and after a renovation we had a large open floor plan for our main room, with five private offices and a foyer. The day Don Boscoe started, the offices and the open floor plan were all absolutely full, so out of necessity, we seated Don Boscoe in the foyer. He was just outside the card-activated security door, next to two waiting-room chairs and a water cooler. The rest of the employees would walk by Don Boscoe many times each day... to go the restroom, to get some lunch, and any time they needed water.

On what was probably Don Boscoe's third week, I walked through the foyer and gave him a how-ya-doing, which he enthusiastically returned. Like probably 50 times in those three weeks, I was walking with purpose and had important things to take care of, but for some reason that day, as Don waved at me, his CEO, with that earnest John Candy grin on his face, I thought, "I should take a minute and talk to our newest employee, this fuck sitting alone in the foyer." I paused and turned fully to face Don Boscoe.

I said, "Hi Don, how is the new job going", as I gave him a top to bottom once-over. Don had a degree in technology, but this was his first tech job. He had started working in a distribution center warehouse during school and had continued to work there, struggling to get his first programming job, until his friend's referral opened this door.

"Mr. Whitney, you had me at air-conditioned office," he bellowed, followed by a steady stream of enthusiasm, positivity, and appreciation. As I stood there soaking in the glowing assessment of our company, working conditions, and my inspired take-a-chance underdog hiring strategy, I noticed a peculiar detail in Don's attire. He was wearing a collared short-sleeve polo-style shirt, which was orange, but not fresh orange, more like 300-

times-washed orange. In the middle of the chest there was a distinct, significantly faded patch a bit larger than a dinner plate. "Hmm", I thought, and my brain simultaneously asked two silent questions. "I wonder what caused that, and why would anyone wear that shirt to work."

A few days later, we reconfigured our offices and were able to free up enough space to move Don's desk into the office proper. As I was passing through the foyer to go home on the day following the move, I noticed a prominent mark on the wall. Where Don's desk had been sitting, there was an eight-inch wide, three feet high rubbery black stripe running vertically up the wall. The best way I can describe it is that it looked like a drag racing super-cycle had peeled-out up the wall. It was three shades darker than Vanta black, a literal visual abyss. I'm not sure if I mentioned, but the foyer was almost brand new, so the walls immediately to both sides of what seemed to be some sort of industrial accident, were perfect, crisp, unblemished white.

"The fuck could that possibly be", I said to myself.

Investigation revealed that Don Boscoe had spent nearly every minute of the three weeks he'd sat in that location, kicking the wall in his warehouse boots, more specifically, his left boot. He had unconsciously transferred a quarter of an inch of rubber from his left boot sole to our foyer wall, thump, thump, thump. I believe when he walked into my office after the mystery of the black mark was solved, and said "I'm sorry about the foyer wall", as he stood there in his boots, I could detect a perceptible lean on account of the thickness difference between the two boot soles.

Coincidentally, the confusing orange shirt had come back up in Don's limited rotation, so after accepting his apology and reassuring him that such things were a normal part of my management day and not to worry about it, I asked about the lighter patch on the shirt. "Don Boscoe", I said, "why is there a giant stain in the middle of your shirt."

"Well," said Don Boscoe, "my roommate's dog was having diarrhea, and it ran into my room and this shirt was on the floor, and for some reason the dog had some of that diarrhea directly onto this shirt."

"I see."

"It came out pretty well, but I had to bleach it a few times. This isn't a stain, it's the bleach mark. To be honest, it's the cleanest part of the shirt."

And so began my training in the Lessons of Don Boscoe.

Months passed and things happened. Don Boscoe proved himself to be both a tireless workhorse, and one of the most complicated employees I've ever encountered.

At a company happy hour, Don revealed that in high school, due to a wrestling team dare, he had once cooked and eaten a small part of a roadkill cat. I know that was a lot, we'll wait here while you re-read that sentence. Just let us know when you're ready to continue.

One of the problems... I said **one** of the problems... with that story was that the typical lead-in to kick it off was the phrase "the time Don ate a cat". I'm going to say this, and I acknowledge up front how it sounds, but *there is some nuance to the actual facts of the cat-eating story* which are not adequately reflected in that introduction.

Our project was going well, and in the Summer of 2006, leadership from The Client, including multiple VPs and Directors, wanted to do an on-site with us.

With an important client visiting for two days of meetings, I recognized that it was possible that while working together in close quarters, some of the rough edges of certain members of our team might reveal themselves. The day before they arrived, I scheduled an employee all-hands.

Knowing that people respond better to visual examples, I scripted several hypothetical interaction scenarios, and had team members act them out. In one, an employee we'll call Kumar, in the role of a Client Vice President, said "do you live in this town, or do you commute from Columbus", to which an employee we'll call Kevin replied, "one time I ate a cat".

In the following full-company discussion, to my great relief, there was unanimous alignment that Kevin should not only have chosen different words, but in the best interest of our company, an important client relationship, and himself, it would likely be better to avoid the entire topic altogether. The next morning, with optimism and excitement, I welcomed our guests to the office.

After a great day of introductions and productive collaboration, we took our guests and the key team members supporting the project to a nice steak restaurant in Columbus. We were seated at a long table with maybe 20 people total, and I was somewhere near the middle. Dinner was going smoothly, there was clearly a great personal connection between our team and each member of the Client delegation.

And then from one end of the table I hear Don Boscoe clearly say "well, there are some things we're not *allowed* to tell you".

At that moment, my *body*, not my brain or my mouth, said the word "fuck". This has only happened to me a couple of times but imagine the word "fuck" was a two-foot-long centipede that was able to crawl up your spine through the hole in the middle of each vertebrae. It takes its time, and you feel it click past each bone. "Fuuuuuuuuuuuuuuuuck", said my body.

"Well... what is it that you're not allowed to say", said a third-glass-of-wine Client Director, because *of course they fucking would*.

Let this play out slowly in your mind, as it did for me. Like watching a bullet being fired at you in slow motion, and your brain has those couple of beats to select a duck-spin-jump response.

Except it's not a bullet, it's a hose spraying liquid shit, being waved around wildly by a clown-nose-wearing psychopath.

"Don... *that's an inappropriate story for dinner time...* but if our guests *insist* on hearing it then...", I said out loud before continuing silently in my mind "because as fucked up as it may be, it's not embezzlement, fraud, or a data exposure, which is what they're going to think if you don't tell them, because not a soul on earth imagines the story you aren't allowed to tell is about *eating a goddamned cat.*"

And then, like an alternate-universe fucked up Shakespeare holding forth at the Globe in the year 1600, Don told his story. And the executives laughed hard and long and loved us so much more.

I worked with Don Boscoe at that startup, and then six years later brought him in to another company. The number of times I've been certain Don has doomed us all is well into the upper triple digits. But other than irritating but relatively harmless blowback that seems only to affect me, or himself comedically, Don Boscoe, and everything under his protective aura, *always* comes out just. fucking. peachy.

While situationally diverse, the Lessons of Don Boscoe are connected by a thematic spine that can be summarized with the phrase "I clearly do not know what the fuck I'm talking about". In the presence of a Don Boscoe, the Laws of Physics become loose guidelines. Up may be down, chaos may be order, and two plus two might equal "pancakes". The Don Boscoes of the world were why shrugs and subtle head shakes were invented. If you are lucky enough to recognize a Don Boscoe during an interview process, may your enthusiasm for hiring them only be eclipsed by your future regret.

Brazilian Jiu-Jitsu as a Template for Reduction of General Dipshitery

I want to make this clear right out of the gate, I'm not particularly good at Brazilian Jiu-Jitsu. For those that know something about BJJ, I started around age 42 and made it to three-stripe purple belt after seven or eight years, and then began to be demoted because I wasn't showing up very often, and my primary instructor, who has been a friend of mine for years now, does not give a fuck about excuses. He's a former Marine who owns a school in Columbus, Ohio, and when you sign up, he'll tell you there's a two-week trial period. He'll also make it clear that the trial period is for *him*, so he can figure out if you're going to complement the school's culture and community, or potentially screw it up. And at the end of two weeks, if he concludes that you're there for the wrong reasons or you're an uncoachable meathead who might hurt someone, he'll tell you that you can't come back. He's actually done that. I've never heard of another business with a policy like that, but... welcome to BJJ.

I have no activity that I'd recommend more strongly for everyone than BJJ. The experience is way beyond grappling, self-defense, "fighting", and whatever else it may seem to be superficially. In a world where it seems increasingly difficult to find great In-Real Life communities, BJJ is like the hulk-on-steroids of communities. Nothing else is quite like it.

In my opinion, there is a single reason why this is true and unique to jiu-jitsu: it is possible to live-spar with a partner at 100%, going until one of you "taps", and do it over-and-over without getting injured. You can't do this in other martial arts. If there's any kind of striking involved, either you cannot realistically apply the techniques, or someone will be experiencing real pain and likely real injury. This builds an incredible level of trust between you and your partners, because everyone knows what will happen if you don't stop in time, or if you flail like an idiot.

I started jiu-jitsu as part of my depression-mitigation process following a divorce when I was in my early 40s. Before jiu-jitsu, I spent a couple of years going to a boxing gym, and I built what I now call "body by depression". I was a hollow train-wreck of a human being on the inside, but on the outside, I looked like Hugh Jackman Wolverine. I realize based on the nature of our relationship, you believe I'm fucking with you, or are thinking "sure, the end of Logan maybe", but I'm really not. I was absolutely ripped.

On one of my first nights, during jiu jitsu sparring I ended up paired up with a 13-year-old kid who had been doing BJJ since he was five. We'll call him Tyler because that's what everyone calls him. As we slapped hands, I made some comment like "hey, don't worry, I know I'm massive and jacked, but I'll be careful not to hurt you". I still remember this: he gave me kind of a confused WTF look, which at the time I naturally attributed to the fact that kids are sort of stupid.

While Tyler had a huge amount of mat time and skill, he was still a little kid who did not have any kind of trash talk game to tell you how much he was going to fuck you up, so he just fucked you up quietly. Imagine a Cuisinart (one of those vegetable shredder things) where you stick in a bag of carrots and a whole cabbage, and with an absolutely straight face, no emotion whatsoever, every time you stick something in, it totally fucks it up into slaw. Over and over again. It doesn't care, it just does the thing it was built to do, and fucks that shit right up.

That night I was a sack of radishes, fed in one by one, and in just about as many seconds, I came out the bottom... no longer recognizable as radish. It's not an exaggeration to say I was over twice this kid's weight, had probably a foot and a half of height on him, and we'd slap hands, and in about ten to twenty seconds, like a fricken spider monkey he had one of my arms extended and was right at the edge of breaking it. At one point after tapping, I asked if he would hold here and please not break my arm and allow me to test it a little more to see if I could get out. Not even fucking close. I was allowing him nothing, I was not only not helping, but I was resisting with everything I had, but because I didn't know what I was doing, it made absolutely zero difference.

Tyler is now a black belt in his 20s, and it's still true that when we do jiu-jitsu together it's like two completely different disciplines, like watching an astrophysics debate between Neil deGrasse Tyson and a chlamydic eucalyptus-gnawing Koala.

I explain this to try to convey a sense of the sparring process, and its function as one of humanity's greatest truth-finders.

Imagine a deep subject matter domain where each participant's understanding is constantly tested by people attempting to use their own knowledge to choke you the fuck out. I don't mean that metaphorically. There are no verbal debates, there is no opportunity to form an opinion and walk away with it unscrutinized, untested and intact. You think you understand, and you "roll" with someone who understands better than you, and soon you're underneath them huffing for air. If there is enough time on the clock, they catch you and almost break something off, so you tap. That's where the argument that never happened ends. It isn't even a matter of right or wrong because it never had the opportunity to be structured that way. There's what worked and what didn't, period.

This knowledge hierarchy translates directly to the belt progression. Each belt level is hard-earned. This is not to say that there aren't substantial differences between practitioners within the same rank, *but*, with rare exceptions, a blue understands much more than a white, and so on.

This is a highly efficient knowledge dissemination framework, because people that don't know what the fuck they're talking about **never** get the microphone, and the experts **always** do.

Picture a scenario where a skilled brown belt regularly train-wrecks her standard pool of less experienced training partners.

Fourth wall break: I bet using "her" there gets an eyeroll from more than zero people, believing that to be some sort of forced-nod to hypothetical equal participation. In fact, I'm referring to a specific friend, who has won gold at brown in a number of world-level tournaments, and who will fuck. you. up. She's also a programmer, but I don't discuss that with her for fear that I'm also less good than her at that.

And then a black belt with impressive competition credentials shows up to teach a seminar. Does the brown belt puff up and constantly attempt to demonstrate I'm-good-too, or interject counter-perspective into the seminar session? Hell no. Do they roll and does the brown belt go 100%? Absolutely. But the outcome will almost certainly reinforce the expectations, and if it doesn't, there will be respectful discussion, acknowledgement of the impressive skills of the brown, and a really-mean-it both-hands handshake.

But nowhere else in life does it work like this, and certainly not in your technology or business career.

No, to be clear, I'm not suggesting we port the jiu jitsu model over to our professional lives and start to choke each other unconscious with our knowledge of Infrastructure as Code scripting. Instead, I present it here as an example of a subject domain with highly efficient knowledge transfer, with the hope we can borrow from it to improve how we learn from each other and make decisions as a team.

What Does This Look Like

A "good" model that doesn't include fights to the fake death should be characterized by:

a) Efficiently enabling the suggestions coming from the most-best experience related to the problem domain to rise to the top and take priority as you craft the plan,

b) Include the ability to surface potentially good ideas from the other dipshits,

c) Create opportunities for the less-knowledgeable people to learn.

Achieving all three of these at the same time is much harder than it should be.

One obstacle to this can be the specific personalities in the team, which can range from "Quiet People" to "Strong Voices", and everyone in between. Quiet People, regardless of their actual level of knowledge, do not like conflict, and possibly even attention, and as such, are inclined to fade into the background. I talked about this in a video, but some of these points are worth repeating.

I've worked with developers whose neurodivergence has both made it hard for them to feel comfortable elaborating their thoughts, while giving them a truly superhuman ability to press the right plastic buttons in the most optimal possible order. They make fantastic teammates, and they're some of my favorite people to work with.

However, these people are susceptible to getting steamrolled in discussions by the Strong Voices. This is not a good thing. I can say this from experience, as a Strong Voice who for a long time thought I had the best ideas because no one challenged me, only later to realize they were holding back all of their genius because they just didn't feel like participating in a Lincoln-Douglas debate about blueberries and watermelons again.

Strong Voices can also be a problem in a team that doesn't include Quiet People. While it is great to have people willing to assert a clear perspective, make decisions, and lead, finding the perfect balance of just-right vs too-much can be challenging. The key thing is to observe and talk privately with other team members to gauge whether the Strong Voices are providing helpful leadership or imposing their will. If the latter, addressing this will require direct constructive feedback, likely with some ongoing maintenance. The good news is that other than in extreme circumstances, you can positively reinforce the overall good that the assertive person brings to the team, with an "and also" reminder to ensure everyone gets time at the microphone and to have their ideas taken seriously.

Assuming you're able to overcome and manage the SV vs QP dynamic, our a-b-c points become straightforward.

Other Tips

Testing is great. Discussion is good, but if it runs too long or gets stuck in a loop, move on with a test. The beauty of technical disagreement is that it's usually easy to have a bake-off. Define a small but relevant scope, a short time box (a day or two), and then unleash the disagreeing parties to prove themselves.

Stay focused. Anyone proposing a path should start by making one or two most compelling and irrefutable arguments and keep the initial discussion on those points. Either the intractable problems, or some potential for validity, will become clear, and you can quit or continue as appropriate.

When you can't agree, bet on experience. If, as a manager or peer, you need to intervene in a deadlock, without a clear and compelling "winner", always go with the person with the most directly relevant experience.

Decide and own. At some point, whether the team goes forward with the silverback or the rookie, it's time to end all debate and invest yourselves in the chosen path. Once a decision is made and the direction is chosen, even the die-hard skeptics need to get on board and support a positive outcome any way they can. Yes, if it goes down in flames, there can be some I-told-you-sos, shame and regret, but until that point, everyone should be 100% dedicated to success, regardless of whose methodology was chosen.

It's The People Connections, People! Connections!

Something every human should know about is the Harvard Study of Adult Development. There are many articles, Ted Talks, podcast episodes, you name it, that have examined this research project.

The original study started in 1938 and followed a class of Harvard men throughout their lives, until death or now, whichever came first. Read about it here: www.adultdevelopmentstudy.org.

I'm bringing it up here to emphasize the most interesting finding, which is that out of all of the myriad statistics the study tracks and measures, the one that correlates most strongly with happiness was *having a great close people network as you age.* This isn't four thousand anonymous connections on fucking LinkedIn, this is about the people that care about you, who you care about back. Your family and your friends.

Again, you really need to understand what this study reveals. Long-term happiness isn't correlated with wealth, position, or other traditional success metrics. It's about your people.

Related to this, technology has a strange role. On one hand, technology allows my distributed family to stay in touch and see each other's faces much more often than we could otherwise. On the other, our devices, our apps, and our games, create incredible isolation. We are losing our boredom-driven hunger for real social connection.

Technologists have a unique relationship to the isolation that can be created by the use of technology, and maybe nowhere more so than the specific case of using technology to create more technology.

Programming and implementation work is isolating by nature. Let's bundle all of this type of work, from coding, to data processing or analytics, to infrastructure implementation or management, to no-code or even design, any work you do alone in front of the glowing plastic box, and we'll call it "building". Anyone who enjoys building is almost certainly lying to you if they tell you they don't love the hours alone just figuring stuff out and trying to make something work.

There was a period, 25 years ago, where I worked 90 to 100 hours a week programming, for a year straight. I was a contractor, and was billing for this time, so I was obsessive about recording the hours accurately each day. I had a notebook filled with dates and hours, and I don't think I've ever seen another physical object that was more clear proof of mental illness. I burned it years ago.

I know plenty of people that have worked long hours, but a 100-hour week deserves some analysis. 100 hours is an average of more than *14 hours each day, seven days a week.*

This is when I was living alone in a warehouse in Jersey City, New Jersey, and commuting across the river to work at the American Express offices. I would wake up before 7am, work for an hour at home, and then shower and take the ferry to be at the office by 8:45. I'd work in the office until 8 or 9pm, grab a box of take-out sushi from one of the restaurants downstairs on my way to the ferry, and then get home and eat while working for another hour or two. My "break" was the ferry ride home, when I stood outside and took some deep breaths of night air while looking at the New York lights and the Statue of Liberty, for about seven minutes. On the weekends, I would do "16 easy" both days and never leave my apartment, which would buy me a bit of time to have a proper dinner or meet people once a week in the evening on another day.

This can be hard to grasp until, god forbid, you experience it, but the difference between a 70 hour work week and 100 hours is as different as having a pet dog versus a T-Rex. It's not just more of the same thing. To do 100, you can do nothing else. No tv, no reading, and certainly no other go-out-into-the-world activities. You have to become a machine of routine, and after doing that for weeks and months, you start to forget how to step off of the gerbil wheel. Doing other things requires that you have the mental space to first *consider* other things to do. This is totally incompatible with 100 hour weeks, both because there isn't time, but also because you can't muster the right maniacal mono-focus if your brain ever wanders to all of the things you're *not* doing.

Almost all those work hours were spent programming, and for the first nine months or so, I really enjoyed it. I ran the code-test-reward dopamine loop a dozen times a day, and for a lot longer than it should have, it felt like enough.

Loneliness is just a different kind of cancer. While that may not be true medically, you should treat it like it is. But... not with chemotherapy, that would create a whole new set of problems. Look, I think we can both acknowledge I may have overplayed my authoritative-perspective-hand with the loneliness cancer statement, but I stand by it in-spirit. Loneliness can really fuck you up, you need to take it seriously in yourself, and in the people you care about. If you say to someone "I've got fucking cancer", they'll be really worried and offer to help, and you won't feel stupid for saying it because it's fucking cancer. But you probably won't say "I feel lonely and kind of depressed", and this is statistically more true if you're a guy. My point here is that, except in the ways they are not, loneliness and cancer are the exact same thing.

Agile, Suicide

The person whose life ended wasn't in technology, but I'm choosing to talk about it here because his surviving ex-wife, who is my friend, and who I've fired twice, I met almost twenty years ago when I hired her to manage... technology.

Tina, we'll call her, for no reason other than this will likely trigger a "fucking... *Tina?*" discussion with her at some later point.

Tina has borne an amount of life-level fuckery that would have killed a weaker person. For the two cases where I was the cause of that fuckery, the two times I fired her, the failure situations leading to that outcome were 90% or more my fault. And one of the first things she said after the second time, when she also in-parallel, had actual cancer (not loneliness, though maybe some of that too, but actual fucking physical cancer... in hindsight this whole section could have benefitted from a professional editor), was that "as crazy as this might sound, this doesn't rule-out my interest in potentially working with you a third time". Again, if I'm in a sim, whoever programmed the "Tina" NPC is an absolute fucking lunatic.

One week after the death-by-suicide of Tina's recently ex-husband, Don Boscoe, who I hadn't seen in six months, proposed that we go to a Columbus Blue Jackets hockey game, in part because Tina, as a long-time season ticket holder, would also be going.

We met before the game at a bar in the neighborhood outside the arena, on a rainy Friday night when the Arnold Sports Festival was happening at the convention center right across the street. For the most-of-you who don't know what I'm talking about, this is likely going to sound like I'm having an aneurysm.

In 1970, Arnold Schwarzenegger won an important body building competition that happened to be in Columbus Ohio, and met a local with whom he decided to partner to create an annual bodybuilding event. It started in 1989, with something like 30 competitors. They kept doing it, and it kept growing, and now it has many different sports, and attracts over 12,000 athletes each year. For three days in late Winter, the air in downtown Columbus smells like protein farts and the streets are full of people in shirts that are way too small. This has nothing whatsoever to do with the main story here but tell me that this context side quest didn't make it better.

Inside the venue, me, Tina, Don Boscoe, and a man that I'll only refer to as "Brick", walked around the lower bowl hallway toward our seats, when Tina said, "hey, do you want to meet my downstairs bartender?", and walked us around a long curved vending counter to a back-side register with no people and a friendly looking woman named Kelly.

Tina and Kelly greeted each other as old friends, and Tina introduced us. Kelly then said, "Tina and I have known each other for a long time... we've talked about everything that's happened...". To which Tina replied, "well, there's been a new development".

"Oh, sweet fuck", my mind said to me.

"Well, is it something good, or something bad?" asked Kelly.

"It's pretty bad," replied Tina.

I don't know how many times you've had the prospect of a friendly social encounter followed by ordering a beer suddenly take a derailment towards a totally raw revelation of a recent suicide with a merry band of dipshits watching, but there we were.

"Best clinch up", my mind said to my ass, "it's about to get weird".

Two things then happened simultaneously.

"I'll have a Bud Light, I'm going to the restroom," are the perfect words said at exactly that right moment by Don Boscoe, who then walked away, while, and I'm completely certain I saw this, the man named Brick instantaneously teleported 75 feet to the line to walk down to our seats.

"I'll fill you in later", said Tina, taking advantage of the diversion to postpone until a more private opportunity, as Kelly poured Don Boscoe's Bud Light that apparently I would be paying for.

"Praise be, I think we're clear", said my mind. "Oh thank god", replied my ass.

Later, Tina snuck us up to the club level where her seats were. We stood behind the top seats for the last period, talked about feelings, talked about how to feel about feelings, more than one of us teared-up. At some point my phone email-buzzed.

I mentioned at the start of this that I knew Tina originally from work. She is an Agile specialist, leading Agile transformations for big companies, and keynote-speaking at national Agile conferences. Re: Agile, she's a pretty big deal.

The email that I had just received was from Atlassian, reaching out after I had made a video suggesting that they don't care about their customers because they're too drunk from their corporate open bar policy. I held my phone up for Tina to read, one of the few people in my personal life that could possibly understand and appreciate how ridiculous this was. Then we spent the next half hour tossing out possibilities and laughing so hard I may have shit someone else's pants.

Our people connections really matter. I'm not as good at it as I'd like to be, but I'm getting better.

And I really hope I get a chance to fire Tina a third time. Or maybe she turns the tables and gets me next round. Or maybe we both stay employed and settle for a draw. Either way, I'm in.

31

Management Semi-Pro Tips

I'm calling these "management tips", because even if you're not technically a manager by named role, if you're the only one in the room that understands these truths, then my friend, you're the captain now.

Remote Workers Should Have Their Cameras On

I have never met another person who prefers to turn their camera on during an on-line meeting. Not a single fucking person.

People who turn it on voluntarily are not turning it on because they want their own camera on, but rather because they want *you* to turn *your camera on*, so they're not talking to a black void. They understand that it would be unreasonable and creepy to expect you to sit there, letting them watch you and have some semblance of human connection, while they remain just a couple of initials in a colored circle.

People who turn it on with strong reluctance, whether they give two shits about seeing people or are in turn seen by people, understand that seeing each other's faces is hugely important when trying to build connections. Do they love sticking their head under the shower five minutes before their first meeting and pulling on one of the three work shirts they keep on hangers on the pull-up bar or treadmill handle just out of visibility in the corner? Hell no. No one wants this, you are not special in your unwillingness to "camera", Betsy.

Imagine an in-office experience where you could check an "I never want to be seen by my co-workers" box during your employee onboarding, and based on this preference, the company would need to give you a windowless private office, and a personal Segway entirely contained in a phone-booth-like opaquely-tinted mobility pod that you could use to go to the restroom or the kitchen. It would have a light on top, which would flash when you activated it to indicate that your pod would soon be opening momentarily, for example, to share your thoughts on a whiteboard, or retrieve the hazelnut creamer from the refrigerator, to alert all nearby co-workers that they must immediately look away or face stiff penalties if you happen to be seen.

This is the same thing as the Non-Camera People.

Spouse: "You look really fucked up again today. You're going to work like that?"

NCP: "Yeah, but I never turn my camera on, so they don't see me."

Spouse: "You've worked at this place for a year, and you're telling me the people you work with have never seen you?"

NCP: "Never one time."

Spouse: "The hostess at *Olive Garden* knows what you look like, and you're telling me the people paying you for almost fifteen months, who you work with every day, could walk past you on the street and not know who the fuck you are?"

NCP: "They would have no clue."

Spouse: "That's incredibly peculiar."

NCP: "Yeah, John Henry quit, and they replaced him with another guy also named John Henry, and it took me four months of daily stand-ups before I realized it wasn't the same fucking guy. I kept asking him for updates on his wife's menopause night sweats and only later found out New John Henry is a 24-year-old gay dude."

Spouse: "..."

NCP: "NJH was cool about it though."

A dataset I'd be really interested in would be the following for all companies and users from the Microsoft's Office and Teams activity logs.

- Employee start and end dates. Microsoft knows when people are added and removed.

- Percentage of total meeting time with cameras on, by individual employee.

- Each employee's manager. With this you could build out the organization tree.

Using this data, we could find out if there's a correlation between a camera-on policy and employee retention. Using this data plus some other stuff, like employee survey data, or team performance metrics, we could find out if there's a correlation between camera usage and employee satisfaction and performance.

I've been a primarily remote worker since 2009, and for many of the years before that. I love not being required to work every day in an office. Overall, for me, it is a good thing. However, the "best" variation for me is to get a few days in an office in-person with my co-workers, maybe two or three days every two weeks or so.

There are a lot of people who have recently completed three years of all- or mostly-remote work, after never previously working remotely for more than a few days here and there. The good things about remote work are obvious right away, particularly for people who have long commutes. Changing laundry at lunch, being there to deal with deliveries or a plumber, more time with the family, all the time you gain back not getting ready to leave the house and then travel for an hour to work, and many others, slap you in the face with awesomeness your first week of being remote.

However, many of the downsides take some time to develop.

You get to know your co-workers differently. For those that don't blur their backgrounds, you see them in their own home, in their own room, with their own personality-defining shit on the walls and shelves behind them, that at least so far, the company can't demand they take down. I worked recently with a Dutch fellow who had exactly one book on a shelf behind him, "Mycelium Running", which I searched and discovered is about how mushrooms, yes, mushrooms, can save the world. Holy fuck, dude, next time I'm in Netherlands, first round is on me!

But... I think the work-social aspects are overall much, much worse in our new remote world.

The amount of stuff I've learned during lunch conversations, or during a break from the plastic box, when I get or unload water and coffee and have an opportunity to talk with people.

Awkward lobby standing and elevator rides. Coincidental two-block walks with people also heading out to find lunch.

Waiting for someone to be done with the milk in the kitchen or offering a handshake or a shoulder or scalp massage to someone in the men's room, like men do all the time, though women possibly aren't aware of this.

And maybe the most important of all, having a chance to talk informally with your managers and manager's managers. I've had many great and career-helpful conversations in the office early in the morning or after hours, or at office happy hour, with people that would be inaccessible in a world of only remote, purpose-focused meetings. But if you keep trying to Teams-call your CEO at 7am on a random Thursday, she's going to have your credentials deactivated, you fucking psychopath.

The people most punished by this are the junior new hires. How do you connect with people and build real relationships? How do you find opportunities to be mentored? It's great that companies can embrace full-remote to attract talent from anywhere with an internet connection, but I suspect that primates who evolved for ten-thousand centuries in small tribes, spending a few hours each day picking ticks off each other between T-Rex attacks, might need more than a few years to transition fully to screen-and-speaker-based relationships without severe mental health challenges.

So, at minimum, do your part and turn on your fucking camera, Betsy.

The Cynics Guide to People Dynamics

Group dynamics create an enormous pressure *not to not know* what you're talking about. That wording is intentional: there's almost zero innate pressure *to know* what you're talking about. Plenty of people sit in hours of meetings every day with absolutely no idea what the fuck is going on and feel no anxiety whatsoever. But, if you have someone like me on your team, who will gladly ask anyone else present at any time, "Trent, what are your thoughts on this", you will witness the sudden impact of the incredible zero-to-a-hundred anxiety in Trent to not say words that make it clear that he barely knows why we're even here.

1. Force Active Participation

Tip one is to use variations of that "like to hear your thoughts" question in every collaborative context as often as possible. Your role and level of importance in the meeting is totally irrelevant, and you should feel free to use this technique laterally to bring in anyone who's been quiet long enough to raise your suspicion of their complete and total ignorance. You could be on a meeting with your CEO, and you should have no qualms whatsoever about interrupting with "if I could chime in for a minute, I think we'd all like to get Nelson's detailed thoughts on this". Not only is there no downside, but outwardly you appear to be the most earnest collaborator in the room, while inside you may be thinking "when this meeting ends, I'm sure as hell not going to waste my afternoon trying to bring Nelson up to fucking speed again".

The key concept here is that you need to *force active participation from everyone in every meeting*. There will be a point in their lives, if everything goes well, where Nelson and Trent can perch their happy asses on a park bench and sit in silence for a whole afternoon blankly watching children cry and dogs hump, but not in our cross-functional project Floof Doofen SWOT analysis meeting, Nelly and T-bone, no fucking way.

2. Draw a Picture

Second, if a person has not written it down, they have no better than a 40% understanding. A verbal explanation, other than for some savant-level geniuses, is not good enough. Note that I said "has not", not "could not". Again, savant-geniuses aside, for the rest of us, actually writing it down, or even better, drawing and annotating a picture, is where you reveal all of those points where you and "we" really don't understand.

In the last few years of my career, the main way I add value to a meeting is that at some point, I will recognize that collectively "we" (all of the people on the meeting) do not understand the shit we're talking about well enough to leave and take action, so *I share my screen with a blank PowerPoint and force the group to help me draw a picture of what we're going to do.* I use PowerPoint because a) I can use words, lines, boxes and pictures, b) I can put shit wherever I want and it stays there (vs a Word/Google doc or wiki-type tool), c) the "pages" structure helps with organization (vs a giant mind map or other boundary-less diagram), and d) we may need to show an iteration of this to stakeholders at some point to validate our thinking. I don't give a shit what you use but keep my entire rationale in mind. It's worth adding that the absolute last thing a manager-of-managers wants to experience ever in their lifetime is even one whole minute of some dipshit dragging around a quilt-sized open-world free-form diagram while trying to explain a project while all anyone else can see are what appears to be serial-killer prison-wall scribblings.

3. Managing *Whatabouters*

"What-aboutism" is a technique many of us are familiar with from years of productive and world-fixing internet debate.

Whataboutism is a slider, and can be good or bad. On one end are the people who ask the critical questions, point out serious gaps in the plan or your thinking, and provide precise and invaluable feedback. On the other end are the buffoons spewing malformed and irrelevant word-clouds like a machine that converts valuable life-time into confusion, sadness, and anger. Most of us are foundering somewhere in between.

When it comes to whatabouters, you *really want* the first type, which we'll call the Helpful Critics (HC), and you *really do not want* the second, which we'll label Fundamentally Useless (FUF). A complicating factor is that no matter what type they actually are, every human on earth that has ever expressed an opinion thinks they're the first type.

To start with, I recommend that you resist the urge to do what I've done in the prior paragraph by attaching these classifications to the *people*. Assuming any readers with a Phd in Psychology threw the book away after the Don Boscoe section, if you're still here you have neither the formal credentials, nor the nearly-limitless human-assessment powers conferred on me as a first-time-author, to allow you to make these kinds of complex and potentially condemning evaluations of your fellow humans.

Instead, I suggest you limit your application of the HC-FUF spectrum to the specific *thoughts and opinions* shared by your team members, rather than as an inherent characteristic of the people themselves. And saying this will hopefully make it easier to get this book "Certified Fresh" by the Society for Human Resource Management (SHRM, which is real and is pronounced "Sherm", ironically like a kid born in the U.S. in the 1950s who was almost certainly bullied in school).

As the HC perspectives are easily recognized, appreciated, and applied, our focus here will be on the FUFs.

FUF whataboutism is created when the intense need to not be outed as *someone who does not understand*, which we mentioned above, intersects with a very real percentage of people in any situation who, in fact, do not understand. FUF whataboutism involves injecting completely irrelevant considerations, and in a project context, it is used to cover up the whatabouters total lack of comprehension of the core concerns by misdirecting the discussion into a more comfortable domain. In a life context, FUF whatabouters are annoying, but in business, they are the destroyers of forward progress and left unchecked, will become the rocky shoals upon which every project meets its doom.

Show no tolerance for irrelevant-tangent whatabouters. I'm clearly a loving humanist, so I don't blame a poor fuck who's found themselves in way over their head. In fact, I applaud the ambition and optimism that allows someone to walk onto the field in a league many levels above their abilities.

However, anytime a FUF whatabouter attempts a vile misdirection, respond with "that seems totally irrelevant... if you keep saying shit like that I'm going to call the squad in case you're having a stroke". Drill into their should-we-considers like you are both handcuffed to the same live bomb and the topic is the choice of which wire to cut.

If the whatabouter's consideration is legitimate, this will be revealed under intense questioning, but it shall not be. Be relentless and totally intolerant, anything short is like striking an "only on Tuesdays" compromise with a playground-frequenting pedophile.

4. Assume They Still Don't Get It

And lastly, for emphasis, *you cannot repeat the objectives, execution process, ownership assignments, and next steps in basic single syllable words, too many times.*

In every conversation about your project, be listening for someone to say anything that is not compatible with the truth and reality, and ask them to elaborate. It may be a simple miscommunication, or they may have slipped back to square zero and no longer have a fucking clue.

For additional study, recommended for everyone, but mandatory for anyone who fancies themselves on a C-level executive leadership track, I strongly advise that you search for the classic management training video "Monty Python and the Holy Grail: Guarding the Room".

The Frameworks and Tools Problem

Waterfall, Agile, Scrum, GTD, etc., you-name-it work organization and execution management frameworks were originally created retrospectively to put words to concepts that people understood intuitively and practically from years of real experience managing projects. They were not true "invention" as much as they were distillations and formalizations of practitioners' knowledge. No one sat down with a blank page and created these models from nothing. They reviewed what worked and what didn't work from their own collective experiences and tried to strip out the bad shit and keep the good.

However, now the learning order is all fucked up. People with little or no practical experience are taught a framework and its supporting tools *first*. As an analogy, sport-specific drills are a great complement and accelerator for sports skills and improvement, but if your first and primary exposure to a sport is a suite of drills, then you don't understand the sport at all. Conversely, without understanding the objectives and challenges of the sport, the drills don't make much sense.

As a new corporate employee beginning your career in product management, project management, or technology implementation, you are given access to tools and trained on a process, both of which are so tightly coupled you might have a hard time explaining Agile without describing specific Jira features and flow. It is possible that you could spend your first few years of employment, "managing work" every day, without understanding the root building blocks of list creation, prioritization methodologies, check back periods, dependency management strategies, and the value of skepticism, to name a few.

I hate saying these words out loud, but we *may* need a new basics curriculum for project management, which would include how to build a good list (and how to tell if your list is good), how project dates work in reality, the criticality of ownership, dependency coordination (with external "loosely controllable" dependencies getting special attention). Strategies for *plate spinning* check-ins, how to recognize that a key contributor is unable to accurately self-assess. How to recognize someone or a team struggling, how to balance comedy, camaraderie and to-the-point productivity. How to use your executive management team, and how and when to run good-cop / bad-cop.

Your job as a manager is made of exceptions... you exist because the world resists simplification. If everything could fit into nicely delegate-able boxes, you wouldn't have a damn thing to do all day. But alas.

Here are some common challenges and my thoughts. Like everything else in this ridiculous book, approach with skepticism. Or adopt fully tomorrow. No wrong answers.

Problem of Consensus

Persistent lack of consensus only occurs in two situations. Either you have bullies and the bullied, or you have legitimate disagreement, likely stemming from legitimate complexity.

The first problem is figuring out which situation you're in. The bullies scenario tends to be chronic, so if you have a bunch of usually-aligned collaborators who suddenly want to die on a hill about something, you probably don't have a bully problem. If battle is the exception and not the rule, you should take that seriously as valuable dissent. See "Be a Decider" below.

However, if for a few team members, there seems to be a never-ending availability of hills worth the ultimate sacrifice, odds are good there's a people-problem. If this is your situation, you should consult resources beyond this book, but my view is that bullies are hard to fix. One important clarification, the word "bullies" is used here to consolidate all manner of chronic steering-wheel grabbing techniques. This can include people who use relatively passive means, like one-on-one lobbying campaigns targeting the emotions of other team members. The core characteristic of these "bullies" is that they manipulate the democratic nature of an Agile team to influence a disproportionate number of them-favorable outcomes. How they do it is not important.

While this may be a losing battle, approach a bully with a very honest heart to heart focusing exclusively on the problems created by this *dynamic*... you're a fool playing the bully's game if you go tit-for-tat on a particular contested point. If that doesn't work, move the bully your oldest codebase and keep asking for more documentation.

Be a Decider

A leader should do nothing if everyone else has it covered. If shit is moving ahead, the machine is humming along, the leader should shut the fuck up and let good be good. In this scenario, the leader's only tasks are to mop sweat from their team's brows and make sure everyone outside the team knows what heroic work their people are doing.

The leader's hands-on involvement only begins in two circumstances, either when the team's machine is broken, or when they cannot find consensus and need a decision made with ownership and accountability. A broken team-machine could be any form of dysfunction within the team itself, or a situation where the team is being pushed past its red line for an unacceptable period. In these situations, the leader is the advocate and defender, of the team as a whole, and of team members, old or new, who are giving their best.

And above all, the leader, when required, must provide decisiveness, ownership, and accountability. Be a person who is willing and able to process the current information, and make a quick decision, while fully owning the outcome.

If there is a ceiling between workers and leaders, it's this single item. We're not talking about under-considered coin-flips. We're also not talking about providing dictatorial direction despite consensus from their team for an alternative path.

We're talking about people who, in a moment when their team is foundering with trying to agree on a path, are willing to absorb all the facts, considerations, and risks, and can make a decision that may affect their team and personal success, while accepting full accountability. This is hard for most people. Either they want to defray culpability by running it by a committee, or they're a sociopath who is comfortable directing with no empathy for the people who would be affected by the worst outcome from the wrong answer.

Decisiveness in the face of risk and/or hard consequences is arguably the core component of real leadership.

The Swanson Principle

The show "Parks and Recreation" gave us the amazing Nick Offerman character, Ron Swanson, a manager who maintains a... *complicated* relationship with his employer and his own role.

While generally Ron is probably not an ideal leadership curriculum case study, one aspect of his management approach that should be adopted everywhere, and in tribute we shall dub "The Swanson Principle", is, put plainly: the *goal of any manager should be to delegate all of their work.*

"Well then, what will the manager do?", you may ask, to which, without hesitation, I reply, as I slowly swirl my management cognac, "not a damn thing".

For this discussion, my assumption is that we're considering an organization using a more-or-less traditional hierarchical reports-to model, where the manager is ultimately accountable for all aspects of the "work" produced by their team. It must also be a team that has unaddressed opportunities, which are only neglected because there are not enough resources to take up the work. This describes most teams in any area within for-profit businesses. If you are in a for-profit business and you have no awareness of the unlimited possibilities for new projects, then the soul of your organization is dead.

Now let us return to our manager that has achieved 100% delegation... except we can't because this person is no more real than the Easter Bunny or a sadness-free Cleveland Browns season.

If you are invested in full delegation, good at packaging up and transitioning ownership domains, have a team capable of stepping up to address the new challenges, who also have available capacity, and have a lot of tasks that meet the qualifications for delegation (for example, do not require restricted-access knowledge), then, at best, maybe you can clear out 50% of your responsibilities. Under ideal conditions.

Under less ideal conditions, which are also called "usual conditions", it's going to be much more difficult. I've adopted and operated with this mindset for years, in fact, it's the same one I use as a programmer (but the "team" I'm delegating to as a programmer is *automation*). And the best I've done is a steady trickle of work moving from me to the capable and ready members of my team.

The fact that this can be hard to do is one of the main reasons you need to push yourself to do it. Elsewhere in this book, we refer to a manager as a "choke point". This is always tied to the foundational truth that one person only has so many hours in a day or week, but how this manifests in a particular situation takes one of two forms.

Either the overloaded manager is an obstacle to growth for their team members, most critically their direct reports who are ready to take on more responsibility, or the team has way too much to juggle, and the overloaded manager is spread too thin to provide the necessary support.

There are only two solutions to a heavily overloaded team, and that is to reduce the work through pushback and reprioritization, or to get more help.

In the best case, you can successfully rationalize getting more help, but keep in mind this has the circular side-effect of ultimately creating some amount of additional work for you, thus making it more critical that you aggressively apply the Swanson Principle.

Priority Management and Pushback

This is important enough to be worth its own sub-heading. Get ready, I'm going to lay some deep thoughts on you.

As you move up the management tree, chances are good you got promoted for shit you or your team *did*, and never for shit you did *not* do. Here's a hypothetical leadership conversation about promoting you.

VP: "What about promoting that fuck _______________?" *Use your crayon to fill your name in so this hits harder. Yes, I left one of these blanks in, be cool and don't tell my wife.*

Full-P: "Yeah, they said they were too busy to do a lot of shit we said was important, so we didn't do it."

VP: "That sounds like they're ready for the big show."

Full-P: "Agreed. Give them the scepter, the corn cob pipe of leadership, and a fresh regrets towel."

I realize there's a lot of nuance and executive management jargon in this example, but I hope the point is clear: this exchange has *never* occurred IRL. You typically get promoted because you rescued a lot of hostages on a lot of planes, not because you had the courage to protect your team's and your own mental health by ensuring good work-life balance.

This is one of the most comedically nonsensical juxtapositions in contemporary corporate culture. From early 2020, with pandemic anxiety and real impact from juggling closures, family, and mental health, through a period of reprioritization of work vs life, and the "great resignation", companies have fallen all over themselves in attempts to re-brand as employee-first organizations. Never has "work" been so obsessed with "life". This is not a bad thing. However.

What seems lost in this transition is the fact that the leaders feeling compelled by a perfect-storm of contemporary pressures to adopt a New Testament meek-friendly management paradigm learned their craft and won their positions with best practices that leaned heavily Old Testament. People who once put whole towns to the sword to close a new client are now reluctantly replying "Approved" to plans for full-remote staff and new roles like Chief People Officer. To introduce and painfully stretch a completely different metaphor, it's all a bit like running into Lord Vader in the eighth-floor kitchen and having him ask about how your family is doing as you notice he's wearing a rainbow flag pin and has cupcake icing on his chest computer. This feels like an unresolved continuity gap.

We're still in an era where the people above you didn't get there by prioritizing their own and their team's personal well-being, and likely neither did you. And that means it's also likely that you don't know how to do it, and they don't know how to help you.

In the holy project trinity of time, resources, and scope, a ten-year-old can understand that if you don't allow more time, and you don't add more help, then you're going to get less shit done. Yet it is a common operating practice for most organizations to constantly entertain five or more "number one" priorities for the same set of workers. The mechanics that enable this are built upon patterns of managing people grounded in the fundamental truth regarding the fluidity of capital and the anti-fluidity of labor. But before some hippie says "Marx", let me clarify that what I'm talking about is not that sophisticated.

As a manager, if I am rewarded for coercing my team to produce X widgets more than I am penalized for losing Y team members, then by god people, cancel your gym memberships and say goodbye to your families, it's time to make some fucking widgets.

How To Fix It

Humor me for a minute and join me in assuming you and your team are not lazy work-dodging shiftless idlers and are good at what you do and deliver a lot of value. In this admittedly unlikely situation, your team will become a magnet for difficult high-priority projects. And if you want to avoid losing good people to burnout, it is up to you as the manager to protect your own and your team's time.

The way to solve this problem isn't by appealing to the organization to be better, it's to decide that you want a garden in your cell, and you're going to do it by any means necessary. You may need to bring in dirt from the yard in the toes of your shoes and fertilize it with your own shit. You can trade some cigarettes with the kitchen staff for some tomato seeds on Italian night. And you'll need to establish that the survival of your seedling is something you'd be willing to shank your cellmate over.

You do not email or respond to chat messages after hours, nor should your team. If you are given five number ones, you ask your leadership to pick one, and if they don't, you Sophie's Choice an arbitrary winner and ignore the rest, no ragerts. (Sophie's Choice is a great novel and hard-to-watch movie starring Meryl Streep where the Nazis make her choose which of her two children will survive. The video game, however, is a disappointing 2 out of 5 stars.)

Delegate everything you can. Push back hard when necessary. Say "no" more. Or keep rescuing hostages and let me know when you've finally won.

Think of Yourself and Your Team Like Superheroes

I'm not ashamed to say this. I did a lot of my people-management growth in parallel to the initial Marvel Universe movie evolution, and the two things were not unrelated.

History may treat the foundation of this section unkindly, and I can understand that. If you're a college student assigned to read this book in a business, technology, science fiction, or comedy writer's workshop any year after 2021 or so, the MCU glow has faded and you're probably thinking "I'm spending X grand a year to read and discuss what this Ant Man 21, Thor 16-talking chump has to say". Fair.

However, there was an era long ago, when the MCU was a few characters whose first great origin story moments were fresh in mind, and a few of those movies were just magical.

Awesome inner-12-year-old moments aside, to the discerning future-better-leader's eye, there's a lot to learn there.

And for aspiring technology or science leaders, it's a damn MasterClass.

The number one challenge with managing people is that they're all quite different, but that's not really how you learn to think about them as you begin your management career.

When you get the opportunity to manage 10, 20, 50 or more people, the organization starts to give a shit about whether you have a more sophisticated understanding of yourself, other people, and what it means to create and operate a hierarchy between the two. But at that point, it's basically too fucking late.

Before you manage 10, you probably managed 5. And before you managed 5, you managed two, or even one. Really steep yourself in this one for a moment, and it makes so much sense you'll start to nod and go "mmmm" out loud.

When you're first given the chance to manage one or two people, almost zero organizations on the planet are going to treat that like you just set out on a path to be a future CEO. You probably got the opportunity because a) you're good at your non-management / individual contributor work, and they don't want you to quit, and/or b) the person or people that are reporting to you are clearly less ready to manage than you are. And your first "manager" tasks are things like approving time sheets and doing all the shit for 52 weeks that makes it possible for you to fill in an annual employee evaluation. These are tasks that *must be done* but are not tasks anyone *wants to do*.

When you're managing a small number of people, you're not there to provide vision, strategic direction, or storm-the-gates motivation. The roles and responsibilities are likely already fixed with limited ability for you to change them (not that you're likely ready, anyway). You are given that opportunity because there are too many heads at the orphanage that need lice-combing, and the people above you don't want to comb them all.

As strongly as it can be stated, this is neither a criticism nor a judgement, of the organization, the lice-headed subordinates, or you (who are someone else's lice-headed subordinate). It's just the nature of hierarchy and delegation at a point in history where management communication is still primitive enough to require a huge amount of person-to-person engagement. In a scenario where one person is managing 20 or more people who have less than 10 years of experience each, that person's only job is care and feeding of the herd. They're the dairy farmer who must bring 20 lactating bovines into the barn twice a day to ensure each is contributing productively. They're not there to whiteboard strategic questions like "shall we breed a flavored-milk cow" or "cheese 2.0?".

Again, no judgement about any job that pays the bills. But our focus here isn't milking-machine leadership, but NFL head-coach… or Steve Rogers / Nick Fury leadership. If you're in tech, your mission will hopefully never be to squeeze 20 identical teats to produce 20 identical ounces.

Which means that your job will ultimately be to become creative, flexible, empathetic, process-knowledgeable, and capable of channeling or even creating, then communicating, vision. So, when and how do you learn this?

Going back to our starting point of "you're now Kyle's manager, congratulations on becoming a manager… no, there's no comp change at this time", the answer is that *you teach yourself*. It doesn't matter if you do a 10-session learning management module, enroll in a class, or get some support from HR. Trust me, you teach yourself. And that process is trial-and-error.

And the biggest problem at that beginning moment, which, barring incredibly rare later inflection points, you'll be unconsciously battling for the remainder of your leadership career, is that your initial training data set is just… you.

Almost everyone's initial management template is themselves and their own story, and to make it worse, this is unconscious, probably more accurately, subconscious.

If you're a type-A workaholic, you're able to recognize other type-A workaholics, and you understand deeply why they're valuable and how best to apply them. If a gregarious, empathetic team-glue-type walks in, your thoughts may be something like "I don't think they can keep up". The unspoken remainder of that sentence might be "...because we're short staffed due to all of the unstoppable attrition". However, left to your natural tendencies, you aren't going to be able to see that this might be the perfect person to help solve your team capacity problem, by solving your team retention problem.

And then time passes, and if you don't trigger many mutinies and otherwise keep your part of the machine turning as well or better than others, you'll be given a few more people and projects. That goes on until either you're fired, you realize you've been in exactly the same role for a decade and accept it or do not (and leave), or you become the CxO of your domain.

Yes, along the way you'll learn, but that won't be some magic scroll you pick up at the end of the prior level that just lays it all out clearly for you. Assuming you're not a sociopath, in the best case, you plod on with an ebbing-and-flowing imposter syndrome, where you start each level with about 10% understanding of how you should handle it and try to piece it together like random escape room clues while the clock is ticking. You move from managing individual contributors to managing managers, and find out that's totally different, like farming and professional baseball are similar because they both take place on fields. Then it's managing managers of managers, etc. The problems are, and therefore the work should be, completely different.

So let us return to our superheroes analogy.

If you have the resources, you could attend the best MBA and executive leadership programs. If you have less resources, you could read the ten greatest management and leadership books ever written. You could have a pretty good leadership mentoring program within your company. All of that would likely be very helpful, do those things if you have the means and opportunity.

However, the single *way of thinking* we're going to talk about here has helped me more than any other resource.

Everyone, absolutely everyone, is simultaneously capable at some things, maybe highly so, and shitty at other things, maybe extremely so. Everyone **can** continue to grow and evolve, developing and accentuating the good stuff, and identifying and reducing the bad. That's a fine ideal ambition, both for ourselves, and as the friend, advocate, mentor, and even manager or leader for others. But the truth of it is that this kind of personal transformation is slow and imperfect and involves many factors of a person's life that may be entirely out-of-bounds for the work context. If your management approach relies on taking the people you have and transforming them to fit perfectly into pre-determined cubbies shaped to fit the people you believe you need, that is some lottery-faith confidence my friend, best of luck to you.

Or... and hear me out... engage your management responsibilities like you and everyone else have both special and potentially highly valuable abilities and knowledge, while also being modestly to severely fucked up. In short, we are all superheroes.

This affects the management approach in a few ways.

- You entirely stop looking at people like they're at all interchangeable.

- You start looking for each person's individual superpowers.

- Most significantly, you begin weighing the superpowers much more heavily than the limitations and vulnerabilities. For example, if you're on your way to fight an alien horde, you're not going to leave Hulk home just because he has a hard time occupying his assigned seat on the flight.

- You start thinking about your team and organization's needs related to who you have and what they're best suited to do successfully, versus where they're most likely to fail.

- You turn the difficult process of assessment and self-assessment into something that can be both much more accurate, and fun and positive.

It's a good time to clarify that we're primarily pointing this lens at "soft skills", including things like communication and collaboration, discipline when it comes to work, ability to understand and explain complicated things, etc., in contrast to hard skills, like competency in a programming language, a design framework, etc. If you need a pretty good Python programmer, and they're not a pretty good Python programmer, then you don't give a fuck whether or not they're also Batman.

I should probably add that I'm not suggesting this helps with every management task. If you're thinking "how is believing I'm Aquaman going to help me create a budget spreadsheet", based on that kind of question, the most critical action for you to take to ready yourself for a potential management opportunity should be to put all your effort in getting hired at a company where the bar is much lower.

Admittedly, I've found it difficult to get other people on my teams to look at it like this, and in my opinion, it's because to them this sounds too simple and silly. "Eric is saying we're all superheroes again... is executive leadership excluded from our drug test policy?"

I agree, it sounds oversimplistic and obvious, but you'd be amazed at how easily this can be overlooked. This is in large part because a roles-first view is in the same logical sequence that you first contemplated the simplistic manage-one-person model, and quite frankly, it's easier, so it's natural for it to become your default.

In a roles-first view, you start with the job. This will be a pre-defined job, and could very likely be a pre-existing job, which means you and others have an example template of someone else occupying that same role. This crystalizes your view of what executing that role successfully looks like. And then you put Susan in that role, and Susan will do some of those things well and some of them badly, but your yardstick is then calibrated to focus on the shortcomings (against the expectations), without potentially detecting the areas in which Susan is finding ways to exceed the prior best-case expectations by 5x, 10x or more.

Let's say Susan replaces Calvin, and performs task A about 60% as well as Calvin, but does task B 300% better than Calvin. Assuming these tasks are even remotely comparable in importance, as Susan's manager, what would you say to her after her first 90 days?

"Susan, that's fucking incredible work. No one, and I mean *no one*, can touch your B. A can get fucked, we're all about B now."

But it's likely that's not how it would go. Susan's manager, who has grown accustomed to seeing what A looks like when it's running great, but has no mechanism to comprehend and appreciate the value of what it means to have 3x B, is likely to focus on the gap between Susan and Calvin's performance on A. They don't understand what it means to manage superheroes.

For those good at connecting dots, an implication of this is that I'm proposing we build our org structure around our specific people. To that I say "yes". Yes, you should.

A foundational truth in any discipline where you're building stuff (tech, construction, carpentry) is to use the right tool for the job. This isn't a cosmetic or personal preference question, but a core factor in all aspects, including effort, timeline, and quality, of the work and output.

To the manager, people are people, but people are also *tools*. If we extend our superhero metaphor momentarily to include the NFL (American professional football), another type of team made up of people with highly specialized physical skills, applying the wrong person to a problem is so clear as to make some choices transparent lunacy for even the least expert observer. As I write this, Tyler Bass is currently the number one ranked kicker in the NFL, playing for the Bills. On that same team is 320lb, 6'5" offensive lineman Dion Dawkins, who is also exceptional at what he does. They both work for the same company, but their cubicles are on opposite ends of the floor. Imagine a scenario where the two men take the field for a critical field goal attempt, but coach has them swap roles. It's a safe bet that Dion's kick won't clear the back of his line's heads from 47 yards out, but stand-in lineman Tyler Bass might actually be killed on that play. They'd have Bills head coach Sean McDermott in an MRI machine within ten minutes of the whistle.

While we're talking about football, you might think that's a good, similar metaphor to apply to our real-world objective of technology management, but I'd argue it isn't. While the diversity of roles and specialized skill sets are very similar, in any sport, there is a *much lower ceiling on the maximum possible success that any single person can achieve or contribute to.* But... Superbowl... World Cup... Westminster Dog Show...?

In technology and the sciences, the right person in the right place at the right time might brain-quake a company-saving security fix, an innovation that means no one goes to stores or movie theaters anymore, or the fucking relativity equation. Under the right circumstances, a technologist's individual contribution could be *a totally, unrecognizably different order of magnitude,* the difference between a firecracker and a nuclear explosion.

How does this apply to an open role, the job description, and the interview process?

It's hard for most companies to create a job description that says "Dunno, surprise us". You need to put down something that represents the hole you're trying to fill and the help you think you need.

But I'd recommend a mindset during resume review and the interview process which is not "can this person do this job exactly as described", but instead, "can this person help us wreck shit, if yes, we'll figure out what fence to put around their role and what to call them later." This should adapt nicely over time, if everyone's comfortable revisiting the open to-be-hired job descriptions after each successful hire. If you start with 20 roles open, hire 10 people, and still think you should have the original 10 roles open, you're not doing it right.

Our modern recruiting pipelines are very different than this. In the service of efficiency, we love explicit hard gates that can easily be automated. Missing a specific degree, a certification, a number of years of experience, and we can toss you out of the process and not waste any more time on you. I understand this.

A strict gate made up of non-optional box-ticks may be a good way to efficiently fill your roster, but this is never going to make your organization exceptional.

Exceptionalism comes from a team that includes unconventional hires, the hungry people, the Don Boscoes. People with an interesting origin story, that wouldn't pass a standard filter, and have a chip on their shoulder about it.

Superheroes.

Be Win-Generous

I don't know if this advice is enough to enable you to beat the last ants at the very top of the pile to become the king of the ant hill, but at every level below that, it is a critical pro tip.

It should not be a secret that personal ambition is required to climb the management tree. Anyone who pretends otherwise is full of shit. If they're in a leadership role, they *wanted* to be in a leadership role, and they did things to help themselves get it. There are plenty of amazing people who *could* lead, who are content with being good individual contributors, and there is nothing wrong with that. But if you want to climb the hierarchy, there will be competition, which means you cannot do it passively. You have to want it.

Our entire lives are spent with external reinforcement pushing us to be recognized for individual performance. I won't list off the examples, but they are myriad. Even in a team sport, a marching band, or an orchestra, while working together as a group is critical, you must fight for your position. Did you ever wonder why there are chair ranks in an orchestra? Is it better for the orchestra that the dipshit fuckwits are further away from the conductor? Yes, because competition within an instrument and honor or humiliation based on your chair position makes the entire section better. The worst fuckwits in a competitive section will be better than the best player in a just-show-up we're-here-to-have-fun cadre of aimless "participants".

This system spits out decent team-players, and the me-first people who end up leading them. I realize these words are cynical and harsh, so feel free to get angry and empathize your way to a CEO role to prove me wrong. Nothing would make me happier. But in the meantime...

A major problem this creates is that leadership is absolutely not about your personal accomplishments. In fact, great leadership is the *opposite* of personal accomplishment. If you have to direct everything that happens, you're fucking it up. Regardless of the outcome related to the objectives, that's *terrible* leadership.

A great leader is someone who finds and supports the people who crush it. That's the job. It's not vision, it's not solutions, it's not rolling-up-your-sleeves. It is entirely about finding and enabling other people who rain threes (basketball... I'm trying a basketball reference).

This is a Wizard of Oz Dorothy's red slippers bit of advice (spoiler: there is no magic wizard, those shoes you got from the witch you killed at the beginning with your house are all you need... such an important message!). Anyone can do this, you have this in you all the time, and as soon as you use it, it unlocks the power of your team, and unlocks the gates that allow you to move up.

It's as simple as this. No matter how much you were involved and needed to guide or steer, for every win, give all the credit to the primary team member who worked on it. Don't say "we", say "they". Take zero credit. Be win-generous.

This is not saying you should reward ineffective dipshits by covering for them. You should not.

Think of this like gymnastics, where the athletes are the stars, but sometimes when learning a new move, they need a spotter. You're the spotter. Maybe you're just standing there with nothing to do, or maybe sometimes you need to catch someone to save their life. But either way, they're the do-er, and you're just the spotter. Except when things go wrong, and then you accept 100% accountability.

This engagement approach has the following effects:

- Very quickly, everyone realizes you're not there to do their jobs. It's up to them.

- Your team realizes that you have their backs. Your first priority is them, and you only win indirectly, if they're successful. This creates incredible loyalty and motivation; they will not want to let you down.

- The leadership above you keeps hearing about your amazing team members. Long before you need to ask for more money or other amenities for your star employees, your manager has heard about how great and critical they are. This point is a big deal by itself.

I don't like the phrase "servant-leader", I think it's disingenuous bullshit. You're not some passive asshole holding the steering wheel while waiting for people in the back seat to yell out directions. You're a leader because you are willing to deal with the hard decisions, make no-good-answer compromises, and battle on behalf of your people who may not be their own best advocates, and you should get rewarded for that, it's hard fucking work.

But as that leader, you... and here's a volleyball reference to sustain the metaphor incoherence... do not spike the ball, you *set up your people to spike the ball*. Even if they don't spike the ball but do something that reflects their willingness to get some floor-burn and take a net-pole to the face, you convince the team to put them on their shoulders like Notre Dame's Rudy after one play, or a Cleveland Browns quarterback after a zero-loss sack.

The best-kept secret of leadership is that it is very simple. The most complex moments are simply hard decisions. Not complicated, just hard, where everyone can't win. But most of the time, it's just helping everyone else succeed. Be win-generous, and in spite of your obvious limitations, your good people will make you appear to be great at your job.

4 |

Your Bullshit-Free Guide
to Collaboration

Finding success while working with other people can be some of the most rewarding experiences of our lives. In no small part because having the opportunity to work with a group of people that runs like a well-oiled machine is such a rare occurrence.

I caught up recently with an old co-worker and friend who was the manager for a lot of my work almost 25 years ago. She's a leader in a well-known financial services company now, and in talking about our careers in the interim time, we both acknowledged that we didn't appreciate how lucky we were to have had such an amazing team back then. There is a huge amount of alignment-of-stars involved in pulling together a great team of people who complement each other and are at compatible moments in their own lives to be able to invest at the same level. I've been lucky enough to have this experience three times (so far), and the most recent time, at my last full-time job, I was additionally fortunate enough to have the wisdom to completely appreciate it.

And now it's time to put hope aside and review the collaboration scenarios that you're likely much more familiar with.

People are Absolute Shit at Objective-Driven Communication

This is another one of those basic concepts that unlocks clarity like night-vision goggles when you're hiding in the dark in order to scare family members. I mean *"if you were to"*... hypothetically. Let's move on.

People are awful at communication generally, and at *communication when trying to coordinate* specifically. This is something we've all experienced from time to time, but what I'm going to try to convince you of here is that this isn't a rare thing you encounter infrequently, but rather the standard operating state of humans.

If you are a competent hands-on technologist or designer, or anyone else who has had a lot of experience dragging a chunk of work into a cave and grinding away at it alone with total autonomy, you've probably come to the realization that, from a pure efficiency perspective, this is the best case scenario. No coordination, no need to come to any understanding with another quirk-filled-brain, you just do the things you know need to be done, in the order you want to do them.

But there is a limit to what we can accomplish in a finite amount of time working totally alone. A thing which is valuable if we have it in the next couple weeks may have much less value if we get it in a few months. Particularly in a business context, *by when* is arguably the critical consideration for any project. And separate from more hands to crank away at the work, there is enormous value in having ideas processed through multiple brains.

So, we assemble teams, maybe just two people, or maybe, god forbid, two hundred, and in so doing, introduce two significant challenges: communication and coordination. Communication and coordination cover everything from agreeing on the exact steps to accomplish the objective, how to execute each of those steps, how to divide up the team, and how to allocate the work. And let's not forget, how to synchronize status and identify and resolve problems, conflicts, and blockers across different working groups and the individual members.

I could make an argument that the best kept secret in business is how fucking awful we are at this. And all our advanced work-management and collaboration products just make the problem worse. The issue with these tools, by way of analogy, is that they try to solve the problem of a monkey being a shitty carpenter by giving the monkey a more powerful table saw.

We have all of these quite advanced tools to record and share every granular detail of the planning and execution process. We could take a pause, probably a full day, to roast each one of these products and share our horror stories about how the tracking solution or the documentation portal or the executive status process or the time logging steps, on and on, were an absurd Orwellian nightmare. We certainly, accurately, gleefully *could*.

While a non-trivial amount of that thrashing would be fair, we love ignoring the equally impactful truth that people just don't fucking use these tools correctly. The reason that we don't use the tools correctly is the same reason behind the thesis point of this chapter: we view the communication and coordination problem as a far-distant secondary concern, and not the primary, above-all-else, critical basis for everything, which, in fact, it is.

If we're trying to design and build software, the "work" is dragging shit around in a design tool, or coding some screen or API route, maybe modeling a database. Yes, we realize that everything else, and here's a nuance, isn't *only* clerical bullshit. However, we don't recognize that clear communication to the point that our co-collaborators actually comprehend us, and we, them, is both *the number one top priority*, and really easy to fuck up.

We expect too much from our fellow self-aware meat sacks, as they do from us. Despite a lifetime of examples that should make it clear we need to lower our expectations, we have a kick-off meeting for some new shit we need to build, run through forty slides, and leave thinking everyone who was there likely now understands 70-plus-percent of what we're trying to do and how we plan to do it. The real truth is that if they got 30% they're likely the greatest brain-trust ever assembled. It would in no way surprise me to learn that 50% or more of all at-work effort is wasted, because people are doing things badly (and iterating) because they don't understand, or are doing things that don't need to be done.

Children make for great case-studies on the topic of communication, not because they're fundamentally worse at it (though they are *somewhat* worse at it), but because they're not nearly as good at hiding their innate incompetence.

I have a couple of sons, they're pretty solid and I'm quite fond of them. But for about ten years after they were three or four, I thought they had an imaginary friend named "Hellifeyeno", based on their standard answer to my standard question of "how did this simple task I asked you to do get so screwed up". To this day, and the kids are now large with mustaches, every time they unload the dishwasher, I'd swear to a higher power that the only way they could fuck up putting dishes away that badly is if they're doing it on purpose to screw with me. Cups in a cupboard that holds canned goods and crackers. Cookware could end up literally anywhere in the house. My grilling tongs were once so well hidden I nearly burned the skin off of my fingers flipping porkchops with two forks like a psychopath.

These are neither stupid nor evil people. They've been family-mission-aligned for at least a decade, but certainly since their combined age became 18 and I started telling them it was time for them to get their own place. Yet they struggle with comprehension of basic project requirements, constraints, and objectives.

Neither you nor any other adult you know is that much better. Yes, you might be extremely OCD and capable of flawless capture and prescriptive adherence to every detail, but your mistake is likely your faith in the dipshits that described what they wanted. If you build what they asked for but not what they need, can we really argue that this is any better?

Communication and Collaboration for Hapless Dipshits

Good news, all is not lost! Empowered with new understanding of this human reality as described above, there are several tools that can help you overcome our tendency toward communication dysfunction.

As a test, if you're around other people, or have a mirror handy, look at them or look at yourself, and say "you're probably following no more than 20% of this bullshit, you poor simple fuck" [while using the hand not holding this book to make a comprehensive sweeping gesture targeting everything around you in all directions]. Now take a moment of reflection, and ask yourself... did that feel *wrong*?

If your answer is "no, not even a little", then you've achieved the proper level of readiness and receptivity to move to the next level.

How to do "Collaboration"

This will be something of a hard-sell, as most people do not tend to see it this way, but I think it's valuable, so [pulls out sword, steps up to windmill...] here we go.

The totality of reasons for having a meeting is a fairly short list:

- You have information you need to share with other people so they can "know" and potentially take action, and it is likely that they will have questions that would benefit from a live discussion.

- You need to understand information or status that can only be provided by other people, and it is likely that you will have questions that would benefit from a live discussion.

- You want to confirm that you or you and the group, understand something (a goal, a project, a plan, etc).

- You need to explain what you're doing to get approval to move ahead, and it is likely that your audience will have questions.

- You want feedback on something, or to brainstorm around a set of questions or objectives.

- Getting people together is inherently good and valuable.

A group of three or more people who show up to a meeting to discuss any topic with nothing prepared, are almost certainly doing it wrong.

Either the thing they're trying to resolve is very simple, so it could have easily been addressed in email or chat. Or, the thing has some complexity, which means it will be almost impossible for these people to have an effective discussion about it using only words, with no written-down points of reference.

The Parkinson's Ramp Project

My dad has been dealing with Parkinson's disease for a few years, and one of my brothers and I determined about a month ago that it was time to add a ramp to the entry door of my parents' house.

At the early ramp-ideation stages, my brother and I had a handful of 10-minute unstructured brainstorming conversations, which served the purpose of exploring and rejecting bad ideas and narrowing the focus to a general approach. And then my brother took that information into his cave and drew up a plan. I don't mean a triangle on a cocktail-napkin, I mean a to-scale, every board represented and labelled, ready-to-build design.

When he showed it to me in what turned out to be a five-minute "thoughts question-mark" meeting, my response was simply "looks great, let's build it", and he produced a ready-to-buy lumber and hardware list.

This is outside of a company environment, there was no team hierarchy or formally defined roles. There wasn't a "leader" until my brother self-selected for the job by investing a lot of time to make his proposed approach crystal clear. As we built the ramp, his plan drove the process, and the only discussion occurred when we had new observations and learning that might trigger a change.

I share this as an example of collaboration perfection.

Under-Prepared Meetings: The Tyranny of the Lazy

There is no such thing as productive, all-parties-equal open collaboration. Unless you're a group of two hundred Amish carrying a barn down the road to Moses and Esther's house, people never accomplish anything by working on the exact same task at the exact same time. The reason people want to have meetings is because they are lazy. I could take four hours today to proactively and clearly record all of our understanding in a few slides or diagrams, or I could schedule a meeting tomorrow and waste five people's time watching me do a shitty job of "talking through it" with flailing hand gestures.

Efficient collaboration should always start by deciding which single person has the best understanding of the problem, the goal, the context, etc., and then, operating totally on their own, that person should write down what they know, and most importantly, *what they think we should do, and how they think we should do it.* To be clear, this initial proposal is not a their-way-or-no-way mandate, it's a well-thought-out starting point that allows the whole team to leap past the aimless-dipshits-talking phase (aka, "traditional collaboration").

Things which are "just true" and non-controversial will never need to be discussed. They'll be written down, and those words in that document become the manual. For the things that *do* need discussion, they can be talked about with the surrounding context clearly established by the diagrams, and the clarifications, truths, and decisions can all be added as annotations to that exact context. When the meeting ends, you can be pretty sure that everyone understands what's going on and what things are still open. And if Kyle misses the meeting because he called-off after staying up too late watching the Browns lose and misery-drinking again, you can generously send him the document tomorrow in a thoughts-question-mark email with everyone else on cc.

What Should I Write Down?

It may be a simple diagram or three bullets in a list. Or it may be a thorough diagram or timeline that makes everything totally clear. The form should be appropriate to your context, but invest your document-creation time wisely. Make sure everything you create has a clear and useful purpose. More is not necessarily better. There is no need to include background for its own sake, or anything that is such a given that everyone 100% understands it and is completely aligned.

My current go-to is a single page swimlane-timeline, followed optionally by separate diagrams for any specific sub-component or process that might not be fully understood by everyone, or which might be controversial.

The power of a timeline-view that fits everything onto a single page is hard to overstate.

- Placing the work and milestones in horizontal swimlanes by team allows you to clearly see who is doing what, when, and in what order.

- Everyone can clearly see the dependencies between teams, and can see work that is happening concurrently and where capacity problems could emerge.

- By attaching everything to calendar-time, you are implicitly estimating each step and providing that in an easy-to-digest visual layout (compared to a long list of tasks). This makes it straightforward to identify areas that may be overly-optimistic.

- If your leadership or stakeholders have questions about pushing the delivery dates up, they can see the dependent steps that can only be abbreviated by violating the laws of physics or gestation, or via adoption of the 16-hour workday. The picture makes the counter-argument so you don't need to.

- And emphasizing this again, all-on-one-page is critical, because our brains can't assemble, visualize, and comprehend dependencies that we're pulling from different parts of a document. I am definitely not talking about opening a standard, noisy project plan or a giant cascading Gantt chart! One fucking page, Brenda!

I've saved people thousands of hours of work with good pictures, and it no longer surprises me when I show a diagram and you can hear the sizzle of people's brains as they come to finally understand what the fuck is going on.

What Should We Talk About?

Whoa... slow down there, Anakin. There's one more critical thing before we get to that.

How Will We Know When We're Done?

The organizer of a meeting should always start by answering the question "how will we know when we've achieved the objective and the meeting is done?" This wording is intentional, as it goes beyond simply defining the *meeting* objective, to the macro objective, which is to get us all out of this fucking meeting asap.

Remote work has made possible a previously unthinkable level of time-management precision. Thirty years ago, a meeting might be scheduled for "the time after the last harvest day and before the frost, at the first light of the beaver moon". Twenty years ago, people wrote their plans on actual paper calendars and confirmed appointments by calling the day prior on phones that were screwed to a wall and which you had to crank. Ten years ago, Roger from accounting might show up to your eleven o'clock meeting thirty minutes late, after being distracted on the way over from the other end of the floor when he found donuts on the table across from Sales and then spent fifteen minutes trying to figure out where the nerf darts were coming from.

But today, with between-meeting travel all but eliminated, we say our goodbyes and drop from one call at 10:00:20, and are on the next one by 10:00:34, greeting largely the same set of dipshits like we're Bill Murray waking up next to that flip clock again on Groundhogs Day.

The time-precision made possible by taking our meetings back-to-back from the same physical spot has conditioned us to increasingly view the connected blocks on our calendar as an unavoidable continuum. We start on-time and stay until the scheduled end, because... [shrug].

In our first weeks of work-at-home, we may have taken a few extra minutes when a meeting finished early to remove our shirts and walk behind our kids or roommates who were also on remote meetings or school, but now our sense of dewy-eyed wonder at the possibilities offered by remote work is dead, and the void filled with cynicism and resignation.

We need to re-socialize that it's an affront to humanity to keep a meeting going because the calendar tells us it's not over. And this starts by establishing the habit of defining what done looks like at the beginning of every meeting.

Related, I'd bet my dollar that Microsoft will make the MS Teams desktop application capable of allowing you to be in multiple meetings at the same time from the same device, before it adds an option in Outlook that will enable you to prevent being scheduled in back-to-back meetings. [shakes old-man fist again while hitting the ceiling with the broom handle, like Microsoft lives upstairs] *You hearing me up there, Nadella*?!

OK, So Now... What Should We Talk About?

Assuming as the organizer, you're now prepared with both materials to drive the discussion, and a clear understanding of how-to-get-done, here are some hopefully helpful additional tips.

- If you show slides, there should be a single, simple goal for each slide, something like "this is what I believe to be the whole BingBong process, so the goal is for you to tell me if I'm missing anything", or "here are the two key changes we'll make to BingBong v1 to get v2, am I missing anything". Don't just show an elaborate picture with no specific ask of your audience. These aren't toddlers you're parking in front of Spongebob again so you can use the bathroom without people watching.

- Do not read every word in anything you show. Ideally you shared the doc earlier, so you can just say "thoughts [insert name of anyone on the call]?"

- Great questions could include: "Here's what seems to be true, what am I missing, where am I wrong?"

- And if there is other shit to answer, decide who is going to own that, and they should take it off-line, do the work, and write it down.

- For every what-should-we-do open question, *say what you think we should do*! *Present a plan*, maybe with two or three options of which you recommend one. But never, under any circumstances, should you only present questions. It doesn't matter if you're way off or don't know what the hell you're talking about, starting *somewhere*, which will become the anchor for a discussion, is much better than tossing out questions that just trigger confused pie-faced silence or worse, invite untethered free-form word jazz.

- And most importantly, speak and ask questions in extremely basic terms, like you're talking to a group of five-year-olds. Don't hesitate to ask what may seem to be basic or stupid questions. I have a friend that recently left a job, and she was scheduled to interview her potential replacement. During the interview, the other person said "it sounds like you're interviewing me, but I was already offered the job by the director", and explained what was said that made her think that. My friend then pivoted to providing training for the rest of the meeting, only to find out later that the other person had not been hired yet, though the director had, in fact, said multiple things that would lead a reasonable person to believe they were being offered the job. *Never underestimate how bad people are at communicating.*

And here are activities which should always be discouraged:

- People talking for a long time about anything that's not written down. If anything that was written down is so incomplete or inaccurate, the person who believes so should say "this is wrong, send me the doc and I'll fix it", and then you end the meeting and only come back when the revised doc is ready.

- Anyone saying "before we get started, I just want to...". No, absolutely not. Unless they're telling you the project is cancelled.

- Anyone being there and never talking.

- People making vague pessimistic blocking comments like "I don't think we have enough understanding of this to move forward". For fuck sake, Susan, just write down a new list of questions.

- Do not discuss anything *now* that you don't *need* to discuss *yet*.

- Do not stay on the meeting just to keep hearing yourselves talk. If you're done or blocked, get off the meeting.

Yes, this is how you should do it even when the thing you'll be discussing is inherently very open, like creative brainstorming for design, script, brand etc. You can have more than one person write shit down before the meeting, so give everyone the assignment of creating a list of ideas, their own simple design mock-up, whatever is appropriate for the objective. Everyone should engage their brains first on their own time, and never wait to start seriously thinking when you all join a call together. Starting from zero with a group is how you end up always doing whatever the most prepared person suggests. And from the perspective of the prepared person, it may feel good that you keep getting to be the leader, but you're just carrying a bunch of lazy or incompetent dipshits, and you never get a chance to learn or be inspired yourself.

Good collaboration is just a lot of individual work with great sequencing.

While we're talking about this, we should also address some other specific types of meeting and "collaboration" dynamics.

The "Walk Through the Plan and Hear Everyone's Updates" meeting.

This type of meeting is borderline atrocity. Thanks to Agile and Scrum, it happens a lot less often than it used to, but for multi-team projects or very large projects with some amount of waterfall project management, it can still occur. This meeting type happens for two reasons.

- As I raised elsewhere in this book, implementers, but equally as important, the organizations themselves, usually do not view updating status in a tracker as equal in importance to actually doing the implementation work.

- Outside of Jira- and Azure DevOps-style whole-team-every-day trackers, implementers make it a point to never really understand how to use the project tracking tool and have no interest in following the data entry guidelines. They realize that *if they are good at it*, the project or product manager, or BA, *will want them to do it*, so instead they just spend the first two or three weeks fucking up the document while peppering the PM with toddler-level questions.

Eventually, the PM just gives up and takes ownership of all the data entry. No matter how often they prod, the implementers never just "send their updates by EOD", so the we're-a-bunch-of-dipshits "Walk Through The Plan..." meeting is born.

The only way to avoid this meeting type is for the organization to grant the PM god-mode powers and allow them to dole out pain and sadness in the form of very early morning and late evening meetings, every-quarter-hour micro status pings, and minute-level estimate and work log granularity. In desperation, the implementation teams will conduct multiple recon and influence outreach sorties with the CTO/CIO, but as long as leadership holds strong and threatens to "give Lauren their home addresses", the collective will shall inevitably collapse, and the team will enter a new age of light.

However (and this is a *huge* however), the thus-empowered PM *must resist the urge to over-granularize the plan*. Being too granular with task details in a plan (vs a Scrum board) can create a large and unnecessary data entry burden on the team. Studies have shown that over-granular project management is the catalyst for three out of every five organically created at-work Fight Clubs.

The Preach to the Choir Asshole

As mentioned above, a fundamental rule of any meeting is that everyone's goal should be to achieve understanding and adequate agreement (on the next step, who owns, etc) as quickly as possible, and once you get it, you all move the fuck on. However, this doesn't always register for everyone.

Let's say that a meeting has been called so that your team can decide who should contact an important client to tell them you fucked their shit up again. If, five minutes into the meeting, Jamal pulls out his pan flute, takes himself off-mute, and busts out twenty minutes of solo Nutcracker themes, the chat thread would light up with inquiries as to Jamal's mental health and "why does he need to be a dick all the time". Not a soul on the call, observing firsthand these facts, would hum, nod, and smile during the flouting, and then challenge *you* for criticizing Jamal and his impromptu concert when there was a bunch of other shit we needed to get through today.

Yet, in an only-semantically different way, we all tolerate the same preposterous and narcissistic assaults on our valuable time nearly every day, at the hands, or more correctly, the monotonous droning-on voices, of the Preach to the Choir assholes.

The defining characteristic of a P2C is the need to keep explaining and agreeing with a decision the group has already made.

You: "So it's agreed, Kevin will email the Outback Steakhouse CISO to tell her that our intern Topher accidentally posted full-access S3 keys to a public GitHub that exposed an S3 bucket containing their proprietary CRM data that includes the salt volume preferences for 17 million Americans."

Patty P2C: "Well yes, as we said, Kevin has the best relationship with the CISO, they [9 minutes later]. It really is the best option."

You: "Yes, yes, we went through that earlier, that's decided, we can move on."

Patty P2C: "And it's not only that, but Kevin is the most familiar with the S3 access logs and can talk about the access patterns [5 minutes]."

You: "Exactly, as we said earlier..."

Patty P2C: "He's also taking his AWS certification test in two weeks, so this [11 minutes]."

You: "We said we agree, for fuck's sake."

Patty P2C: "I could understand, though, if a few people weren't totally onboard originally, because [a complete, robust counterargument to the decided direction, 14 minutes]. So, while that's not my opinion, I think we can all see how it's also a *valid* opinion."

You: "JFC, Patty," shaking head slowly, "Jay. Eff. See."

To address the P2C problem, you first need to recognize that this is a hard-wired personality trait. You're no more likely to convince them to abandon this behavior than you are to help a Cleveland Browns fan understand that not all football spectators are perpetually consumed with suicidal thoughts.

While I normally recommend very direct engagement, in this case, having a one-on-one with the P2C offender where you constructively recommend that they do more shutting the fuck up so that the rest of the team can start to stop not wanting to work with them, is likely not going to go as well as you hope. Instead, I propose the following plan.

Hire an actor friend to attend one of your meetings that includes the P2C offender. If you don't have an actor friend, call any number in Los Angeles and ask for an actor.

Before the meeting, instruct your actor, who we'll call Jessica, to wait until the P2C launches into their second or third re-hash, at which time they should interrupt and say, "are we all just going to sit here and watch Patty *get her jollies* from repeating the same information over and over?" Exactly those words, and most importantly, it must refer to "jollies".

At that point, you break in with, "Jessica, let's take this off-line", and cut the meeting short.

The next day, kick off the meeting with a reference to the prior day's incident, saying, "Jessica will not be returning; regardless of the accuracy of her statement about Patty's tendency to waste time by preaching to the choir after the decision has already been made, there is no place for the j-word in our meeting or at this company".

You may need to repeat this process four or five times, and then once every six months thereafter to prevent recurrence.

Also, more broadly, let's do our collective best to normalize the use of the word "jollies" in professional communication. And before you ask, the means *is* the end.

The One-On-One

Of all meeting types, this is the one with the largest potential value range.

Two people speaking only with each other is both the most and least economically logical meeting type. Obviously, a meeting with the entire executive team is going to cost the company more than any two people talking, but the maximum potential value from only two people talking is that when it's over, exactly two people understand and are aligned on what the fuck is going on. That seems... limited.

But the one-on one is also where real people connection happens. People confide in each other, saying shit like "transparently..." or "just between us..." or "let me first say that I really like Taylor as a person, *but*..." and then sharing their exact and honest perspective, which can be very valuable.

The Sprint Demo

Sprint demos are good. I can see why you might anticipate that I'm getting ready to rip the SD a new one, but no.

There are three potential objectives for a sprint demo.

- Give developers a chance to present, with the goal of helping them get more comfortable presenting.

- Give stakeholders a heads-up about progress, what's being released now, and generate some kudos for the team.

- Force the developers to prove that the work is truly done.

Controversial opinion, the last is by far the most important objective, followed by #1, then #2. In fact, if you never invited stakeholders to the sprint demo, so it was just the working scrum team, addressing only 3 and 1, that would be perfectly ok with me.

As I was first exposed to Agile, the prove-done point wasn't said explicitly, but was strongly implied by some of the demo expectations. 15 years ago was a far more primitive time related to code integration and deployment. Everything about building and deploying was much, much more of a pain in the ass.

Given that a goal of Scrum is that the work is truly done at the end of the sprint, which means it's tested and deployable, one of the demo rules we used at the time was that you could never demo your work from your local machine. You had to use the QA environment, or at least dev (and you would definitely get stink-eye if you used dev). Whenever someone demoed from localhost, it meant that coat of paint they finished right before the demo wasn't dry, the features were just barely functioning, and that there might be a very large amount of work to do to get it in shape to be promoted and deployed.

One thing I observed was that the whole Agile process worked 50x better for teams that adhered to the done-done rule (vs "done-but") and enforced it by using the sprint demo as a check, where you needed to prove your code was truly complete by demoing it off of a ready-for-deployment environment. The process didn't require negativity, shaming, or executions, it was enough just to create the culture where this was the expectation.

This affected the quality of estimation, and the reasonability of the amount of work taken-up by each developer. There were far fewer, almost zero stories that would get carried over to the next sprint, and because no one spent the first days of the next sprint fucking around finishing up or dealing with deployment surprises for prior-sprint stories, they were set up for success for the next sprint too.

In contrast, every time I've seen a team where the top priority of the sprint demo is anything other than that accountability checkpoint, all those other things are problems too. A lot of carry-over, bad estimation skills, and an overall "soft" approach to Scrum.

One other pro tip: yes, this is also enforced for non-UI work. *Every member of the scrum team should show something visual at the sprint demo.* If your work doesn't have a UI, make two slides of something relevant to what you did. It could be screenshots of code, some DDL, a diagram, a gif of a process working in a command shell, statistics of what improved before and after your changes, it doesn't matter, it just has to be *something*. It does not need to be clean and fancy, don't waste time on pretty slides, just put some shit on a screen to show your team. Trust me, this is good.

Farming vs Hunting

As an analogy, *hunting* is a task that you can accomplish from start to finish at any time you choose, whereas *farming* includes external dependencies that are out of your control, which make it impossible to complete without longer-term planning, coordination with others, and some amount of waiting.

At the beginning of your tech career, your work will primarily be *hunting*. You'll be assigned implementation work like rounding or unrounding the corners of a button for the ninth time, or figuring out how to fit forty five columns on a one-page report without using 5 point type. You will start that work and complete that work, with no input from others beyond the words of comfort they share when they hear you sobbing quietly at your desk.

As your career progresses, and as you pick up more management responsibilities, you'll encounter more tasks and projects that benefit from a *farmer* mindset.

The essential trait of the farmer mindset is to first respect and later harness the power of *time*. This is a very simple concept, yet while it's crucial for success for all but the most basic types of work, in my experience, programmers and other tech implementers, and often their managers, don't understand or apply it very well.

Hunting tasks are straightforward: you determine that a thing needs to be done and you do the thing. However, once the project has external dependencies, like requiring a new server to be set up or a new deployment process configured by another team, obtaining answers to questions from stakeholders, getting a file of user accounts to create, getting a vendor contract signed, etc., literally anything you cannot do entirely yourself or within your core implementation team, completing the project within a predictable time period becomes significantly more complicated.

And unfortunately, what typically happens when people haven't developed the farming tool box yet is that they procrastinate and ignore these items, which is the worst thing you can do.

Realizing that the dependency tasks are fundamentally different is the first step. The second step is to take full advantage of the *power of time* by starting the farming process on those tasks right away, before you do anything else.

To be clear, I would much rather do work that I can sit down and complete end-to-end myself. Spending time to formulate a request in a way that you're certain the other person will understand and not fuck it up is much less enjoyable than just doing a task yourself. Even if they understand, you'll likely need to ping them multiple times to ask/beg/push them to get it done, and have to deal with all of the unpleasantness that will ensue if they drag their ass, don't do it at all, or fuck it up. The collaboration process is why our ancestors evolved tear ducts and first tried smoking plants.

At this point when I have a project with tasks that depend on other people, the first thing I do on day one, before starting anything I can complete on my own, is to begin farming. I make the requests as early as possible for those dependent tasks, "planting the seeds" that can begin the growing process before I turn my attention to other things. And, pro tip: this gives me the ability to set due dates that are well in advance of when my project actually needs those items for it to be successful.

For Example, This Book

I've never published a book before, and "self-publishing" means that I needed to figure out, or get help figuring out, how to do or coordinate a lot of tasks that I had zero experience with previously.

Writing is a *hunting* task, and the only thing between zero and done is my ability to dedicate a lot of my own time to work on it.

However, most other steps of self-publishing are *farming* tasks. For example, finding, evaluating, and learning how to work with a printing company, and understanding the lead times and logistics for printing and shipping.

Even before I opened the Kickstarter campaign that formally launched the creation process for this book, I made a list of every major dependency-task, like printing, eBook distribution, interior and cover design, and how to create and distribute an audiobook, and then started research on each of these. Cost, timelines, the specific steps to do the work. I wanted to be sure I understood what I had to do and roughly how long it would take before committing to a delivery date on Kickstarter. Note that "writing" isn't in this list, because that would just be on me to do, and was totally in my control.

As soon as the Kickstarter successfully closed, in parallel to writing every day, I continued my research by doing small tests on my selected printing platform. I would load in the book document as it was and see what was working and what look fucked up. I tried the platform's do-it-for-you design templates, to the point where I found a formatting bug (stripping out my extra "pause for dramatic effect lines") that caused me to open a support ticket. This was open and unresolved for three weeks (*Calendar Game...* see below) before I decided to abandon their builder and start the new research process of doing all formatting in Word and submitting a print-ready PDF meeting their specifications.

This was all in-parallel to the daily writing. I much prefer the hours spent writing, but I realized that the printing and logistics side contained dozens of land mines that could fuck me later. The central consideration is the time required for print-ship, and the fact that rushing either of those significantly adds to cost. The earlier I was ready to submit the first test, the easier it would be to let it run on the slowest-cheapest track, yet still be able to get in another test without pushing the final print date back.

In the *Miscellaneous Tech Topics* section later in the book, I stress the importance of "Integrating with Existing Code Early". A perfect example of this in the book process was that, once I switched to the "design it in Word" approach, I stopped writing for a day or two while I got the formatting set up exactly like I wanted to print, using paragraph styles, setting the final page size, getting the headers, footers, ToC all set up correctly, etc. I did this so that *every hour I spent writing after that would also be a passive, ongoing quality check of the "final" formatting*. And of course, since that time I've found a bunch of formatting fuckery while writing. And in spite of working like that for weeks, when I printed the first test print, there were two page number fours. Fortunately, thanks to the power of farming and early integration, I won't need to deal with a thousand emails from you jokers trying to open a sev 1 defect ticket for an extra page four in production.

Unlike the hunting tasks, which can be a larger block of contiguous work for you, the good news is that properly managed farming tasks tend to be a number of sessions of small amounts of work spread out over time. "I don't have to do all of this shit myself", you might say out loud to give yourself hope, "I can just ask these other fucks and wait".

We'll talk more about this below, but calendar time can either screw you, if you procrastinate dependency tasks and try to grow your pumpkin in a day, or it can set you up to look surprisingly competent, if you use it to it's maximum advantage. It's also a wonderful tool to aid you in coping with unhelpful or lazy dipshits.

The Calendar and *Ball is in Your Court* Games

To be clear, the goal should always be to get stuff done. Unless it's something that's going to fuck over humanity or the world, in which case you should resort to outright sabotage or stall like a motherfucker. But in most situations, it's safe to start from an assumption of best intentions and be prepared to lend your wholehearted support.

But there are plenty of people out there who are not similarly motivated. Every now and then, you come across those teams or individuals that have made *not accomplishing anything* their life's work. In this section, we look at two tactics to defeat those useless road-blocking fucks.

The Hammer

Before we get into the techniques, we need to consider the foundational threat behind them, which we'll call the "Hammer". If you're reading this book while incarcerated or employed by Oracle, it's possible that the Hammer is an actual hammer. In most other cases, however, the Hammer is a metaphor for a dire consequence, such as termination of employment, or even worse, an unshakable professional stigma without the advantages of termination, advantages such as severance, unemployment benefits, and permanent authorization to keep not doing that thing that you were fired for not doing.

Possibly more motivating than a stick-Hammer is a Hammer that has the ability to withhold all of the carrots, maybe some or all of a bonus, or the opportunity to work on the most interesting project, opportunity to be promoted to a new role, etc. So, to simplify, let's define our Hammer as the threat of a *highly undesirable outcome* for an individual or a team. Or, for those poor bastards at SalesForce, an actual hammer.

Before you apply the Calendar or Ball is in Your Court techniques, you need to make sure you understand the relevant Hammer. It's extremely easy to misread Hammer dynamics and end up invoking one that is also swinging at *you*. A scenario where the Hammer-swinger might say something like "I don't give a fuck about why it didn't get done, you were using Agile, it's everyone's fault" is not something you want to discover late in the game.

A leaking lifeboat that you're also on is a perfect example of awful Hammer dynamics. If the three other dudes aren't bailing, you are long past what's "fair"... bail harder, motherfucker! And if you are lucky to survive long enough to put cannibalism on the table, you'll be the one that's too stringy and tough from all the hard labor, while those three lazy, presumably former salespeople fucks, will be soft and marbled like wagyu beef. But I digress.

Playing the Calendar Game

For those of you that haven't mastered this technique yet, this is one of those things that's been right in front of you all the time, but sometimes it takes hearing someone else say the simple thing out loud to have it click.

For every task, there is always an unspoken gut-feel how-long-should-it-reasonably-take timeline. For example, if something requires actual work, like coding a thing, writing a document, etc., and the person who owns the work says "done" ten minutes after the request, by the gut-feel timeline, absolutely anyone would likely say "holy crap, that's amazing!" If it took the do-er a day or two to do that task, our gut-feel would say "reasonable, thank you". And so it goes, as the elapsed time gets longer, eventually our expectations move from "that should probably be done by now", to "definitely late", to "what the fuck is going on over there".

In addition to allowing the team to monitor overall team capacity and plan workload, the purpose of time estimates on tasks that are closely managed in a project plan or sprint board is to get the person or people responsible for doing the work to take a moment to think about it, and then commit to a somewhat fixed length of time to get it done. This is essentially a contract between the do-er and the team or manager. If we accept the estimate as reasonable, we don't need to keep asking "is it done yet" and pressuring the do-er for updates. We can just wait until the delivery time has exceeded the estimate, or ideally, the thing just gets done.

However, many tasks aren't formally tracked in this way. For example, things which your manager owes you, like an answer about your comp change, requests that cross teams which aren't managed in a common project document, or requests between organizations or in your personal life. In these cases, a mistake made consistently by people who don't play the Calendar Game, is to accept a "yes, I'll take care of that", without following up with a "by when?"

Pro-tip: in the absence of a proposed response date from the other person, calculate what seems to be a do-able deadline, *and add time to it*. If a week seems very reasonable, suggest two weeks. For something easily done in two weeks, suggest three or four. Any chronic procrastinator is going to be stunned by your incredible charity and jump at the chance to lock in an absurdly low delivery expectation.

And regardless of how you got to the date, after the conversation, send an email to the do-er, "looking forward to getting X by date". They will likely reply, "thank you, appreciate your patience", thus signing the deal in blood and sealing their fate. With the trap set, the waiting begins.

During this period, you will largely do nothing. If the outstanding task is something that shows up in any kind of formal status, for the first 50% of the agreed time period, make sure it's in green and marked on-track, to establish for the key stakeholder observers that you're a good partner, and that you believe in your do-er, and fully expect your date will be met. If there is no formal status report covering this task, then follow Stacy's expert lead, and create one! Make a habit of sending it to everyone, and no one will mind... your do-er will even thank you, because high-visibility green-status is love.

For the second half of the wait-period, move the project to yellow, and in the status or notes slot, add "dependency, waiting on [do-er's name]". Do nothing else. Except possibly ignoring requests to meet with do-er about creating a more focused distribution for the status report.

On the morning of the day before the agreed due date, reply-all on your original contract email and say, "Hope we're on track, excited to move this ahead, should we schedule a hand-off meeting for tomorrow?" And later in the afternoon, send out the status report with this task clearly in red, with the note "BLOCKED by [do-er]".

This will trigger one of two things from your do-er. Either a "yes, I'll send an invite", or the releasing of your recipient's bowels and probably a "fuck" or two. To be clear, the first response should not be interpreted as any indication that an iota of progress has been made on your request. "I'll send an invite" is the cagey reply of a seasoned, Teflon-coated procrastinator who is well versed in Calendar Game tactics and strategy. You're playing a master, and it's even more critical that you adhere to the following plan exactly.

Because our audience is engineers, or engineering-adjacent, I'll continue my recommendations in the context of a potential software solution.

Something I struggle to understand is how Microsoft has tried unsuccessfully to build phones, which are legitimately really hard to do well, like three different times, but we still don't have Microsoft PowerPing in Outlook. Anyone on the Office team could program this in an afternoon and forever change collaboration dynamics and save us each three or four hours of work every day.

Simply tag any outbound email requesting *anything* to activate PowerPing, and leave all of the follow-up management to ten lines of code, which scans your outbox for open requests, and re-forwards the same email chain with one of the pre-created messages. This would include the morning-before-deadline "excited, meet tomorrow?" email, and continue with the following after the date was inevitably blown.

"Hi [insert name of unresponsive dipshit], just following up on this. I know everyone's really slammed right now, but it would be great to get status. Thank you!"

"Hey, happy Monday [name of sandbagging fuck], just wanted to bring this to the top of your inbox again!"

"Hi [dipshit's manager, now in To line, with everyone else, including dipshit, still on cc], is everything ok with [dipshit]? I've been worried because I haven't heard back about the thread below."

Yes, you occasionally might get a sorry-been-battling-cancer, but that could also be handled by PowerPing. On the do-er/recipient side, simply set your non-public status, and PP can drop that guilt-bomb on each of your persistent and heartless colleagues after the second or third ping.

Six months after launch, something like 60% of corporate communication would just be PowerPing talking to itself. Outlook product team, hit me up and I'll send over a BRD.

In summary, to make sure we're all understanding this very real and profoundly effective strategy, the Calendar Game relies on exploiting a fundamental limitation of the human brain, namely that our perceptions of far-future calendar time related to "reasonability" and "feasibility" are completely fucked up. If you enable someone to schedule something they don't want to do far enough outside of the immediately-worry-about-it window, they'll say "absolutely" and then proceed to help you document both your incredible reasonability and patience, and their blatant failure to execute. You end up with a clean, date-annotated email history, to be used if and as required to bring in the Hammer and either move the task ahead quickly or take Player 2 out of the game.

The Ball is in Your Court Game

BIIYCG is a subset scenario within the overall Calendar Game process. The analogy comes from any game where a ball, shuttlecock, a heated potato, or apparently in early civilizations, a coconut or human head, goes back and forth between two sides, where success is measured by not having the object land on the ground on your side, before it lands on the ground on the other side.

In our task-execution Calendar Game, having the "ball" be on your side of the court means that you currently own some sub-task or next-step that, regardless of who was the original do-er, effectively makes *you the blocker*.

Experienced procrastinators use this all the time because they're so committed to playing for a run-the-clock-out tie… stalling is winning. They have done the level-of-effort math to determine that spending a little time making a request for information could allow them to avoid a huge amount of work doing the actual task. You only need to deploy the "great, but we'll really need you to send a requirements document and a business case before we get started" a few times before you'll see the incredible effectiveness of this tactic when you hit the procrastinators lottery and have the requestor fade entirely away. To be clear, the procrastinator doesn't want the requestor to abruptly cancel the project, because it being in open status but completely blocked allows the procrastinator to keep describing it as something they're "partnering on", allowing them to ensure their plate always looks full to their own manager, and avoiding the situation where, much like blank space on a child's plate, they attract the corporate project equivalent of peas or Brussel sprouts.

Another Ball is in Your Court tactic from the procrastinator playbook, and the one that really grinds my gears, is to *propose a meeting to clarify.*

It is incredibly easy to fall into the meeting trap, because in the context where someone raises it, it sounds... *reasonable.* Part of what makes it so insidious is that if you respond to a seemingly innocuous meeting proposal with "go fuck yourself", in spite of that being the precisely appropriate response, the 1...e5 to their 1...e4, it may not be accepted as such in your work environment, to the degree that, and I can't believe I'm writing this, *you* might be perceived to be the asshole. I'm supposed to cheerfully click the accept button like you didn't just shorten my life by an hour, Nelson, you life-stealing fuck?!?

Agreeing to the assertion that a meeting is required to move the work ahead is checkmate from the perspective of the procrastinator. If a written answer or document *could have* provided the information to unblock and move ahead, you would have proposed that. By agreeing to the meeting, with all its inefficiencies and logistical complexities, you're implicitly acquiescing to the view that the **only** way to move ahead is to *hash-it-out in a meeting.* There's no going back. And you've now polluted what was a pristine black-and-white email record of clear obligation and ownership with a swamp of unrecorded conversations, mis-remembered details, and revised commitments.

[This is me, after you accepted that meeting, slow clapping your opponent while staring you right in your eye-holes and shaking my head in slow, methodical tight-lipped judgement. You fucking biffed it, pal. Biffed it good.]

Do you realize how many ways there are to delay a meeting or prevent it from happening altogether? Invite a lot of people, and it's impossible to schedule. Identify must-be-present stakeholders, particularly executive leadership, and that invite is a factory of same-day cancellations, with the earliest reschedule opportunity at least a week out. And then you finally have the meeting and the only thing you can agree on is that someone "needs to prepare a document then we'll regroup next week... wait,

I'm out next week. I'll look at my calendar after we drop and send some later options." Liar.

If I wanted to use my skills for evil, I could make one initial 30 minute quick-alignment meeting ping like a pinball through a hundred people's calendars for a solid year and accomplish absolutely nothing other than hitting the company's alcoholism OKR. Tip: add an alcoholism OKR, because regardless of how the year goes, you'll hit that one. Cheers!

To train yourself to react without hesitation with the proper level of alarm, I propose doing the following drill. Get a partner who's capable of administering the consequences I'll describe shortly and stand facing each other in an isolated forest clearing or on the empty roof of a forty-or-more story building. Have your partner say phrases like "let's connect on that tomorrow", or "we should circle back on that with the larger team", or "I think we need to bring Tiffany in on that", and immediately after, before you can respond at all, have them slap the living shit out of you. They can also use pepper spray or play a few bars of jazz.

The goal of this exercise is to calibrate your meeting-proposal reaction to a level of visceral aversion so extreme that your fight-or-flight response kicks in automatically and either you run away screaming, or you square up and prepare to introduce mister-connect-later to these hands. At the very least, you won't reflexively stammer an "ok, sounds good" that causes your day to end, yet again, with water-got-cold-but-I-can't-stop-crying bathtub time.

To those of you following closely, you'll already recognize the appropriate countermeasure: *always force it back to the email chain.*

Procrastinator: "Why don't we bring the team together and get all of the answers at the same time."

You: "How about you send questions in email? If it will help, I can send a spreadsheet with column A populated with 1, 2, 3, 4, and you can use column B to write the corresponding questions."

P: "We might have a hard time asking questions if we don't know every possible detail of your requirements and every possible usage scenario."

Y: "Great point. I'll resend the requirements doc, and add another spreadsheet named Questions About the Requirements, and you can fill that in too."

I don't care how long this goes on or what crazy shit you have to say to avoid the meeting, but your bar needs to be life-and-death. You need to keep going until your procrastinator has nothing left but to work in-writing or say, "I have no ability to ask questions in any other way than with my mouth". Give no quarter, take no prisoners, and above all, by God, take no meetings.

Some additional closing tips:

- Never get into an argument. You're not the Hammer. "Sounds good, by when, write it down", and the rest will take care of itself.

- Slack or Teams chats are not equivalent and have many of the same problems as meetings. They'll get messy and full of a bunch of unrelated stuff. If your time-for-the-Hammer endgame email is a patchwork of screen shots, you're going to look more like a serial killer than a collaborative partner.

Expert Calendar Game players, facing off against each other, often end up in the surprising and somewhat awkward situation we'll call "actually getting shit done". If the requestor and do-er fall into an aggressive Ball is in Your Court battle, it's inevitable that they'll end up hyper-cycling back-and-forth through every blocker, and the next thing you know, they'll accomplish the original task. They do that a few times, and the entire project is on track, and maybe even delivered early. My point here is that you need to be careful *fucking around* with these techniques, because if the whole org adopts them, you may *find out* that none of you are, in fact, incompetent dipshits.

How to Negotiate with Your Manager

Assuming you genuinely like your company, your manager, your team, your role (or the role you're trying to negotiate to get), always start by making that as clear as possible. From the manager's perspective, knowing that you are happy, *except for this one thing*, means that you have reduced the totality of shit they need to worry about with you to trying to satisfy that *one thing*. "And" is a 10x complicating factor. Give them exactly one thing they can do for you to move you from yellow to green, so they can stop worrying about you and move to the next dumpster fire.

OK, so now they're working through the problem of satisfying your one request. In all but the most lunatic companies, the main obstacle is going to be *parity*. Is what you're asking for comparable to what other people in similar situations (role, nature of responsibilities, criticality, specialized skills, track record, experience level, etc.) are getting?

Generally, if the answer to that is "yes", this may wrap up quickly with a successful outcome.

However, here are what I've found to be complicating factors:

Your market value is significantly higher than your current compensation

This happens often in tech, because a lot of the hard skills have a very clear current market value, and a lot of people who like doing tech don't like changing jobs, which means they may have come in at low comp, built significant high value skills, but their raise history hasn't kept up with that.

To be fair to your employer, this is a legitimately sticky problem. At some point in the approval chain, it's likely to move out of tech into finance, and it's often difficult for non-tech to understand how it's possible that you started at X, and four years later you're making 1.5X but your skillset in the market is getting 3X. Why I say this is legitimately problematic for your employer is that to give you what you believe you're worth, they must rationalize how you were happy here for four years, you were OK doing the job for 1.5X two weeks ago, but now you'll quit if they don't double your comp in the next month. I hope it's clear why that would be a problem.

In this situation, if you aren't willing to continue to compromise on comp for other reasons, like you don't want to go through the hassle of changing companies, you like other things about the role and team, etc., you're going to need to at least go get an offer for the amount you're looking for, and you may need to just leave. This is one of the most frustrating situations as both an employee and a manager, because if you're right and you leave, they'll end up spending the amount you wanted for your replacement and take a huge knowledge-drain hit that they wouldn't have taken if they just paid you. But while we're on this topic, there are a few other points to keep in mind:

- You may be the big fish in the small pond at your current employer, but just because you know that one critical app inside and out, doesn't mean your resume and interview skills are at the level of other people *outside your company*, which is required to get that top market rate. Particularly if you've been at a company for a long time, you may be great at *the way they do it*, and then find you aren't up-to-speed on the must-have latest bullshit-this and bullshit-that, which the other companies are looking for. Of course, you could learn, but that doesn't mean you'll get the job offer. Remember, the market-rate comp question is the *market* rate, and for it to apply to you, you need to be positioned to *perform well against competition in the current market.*

- Frequently, high comp correlates to high employer expectations and high stress. If you've been at a company for a long time and you like it, it's extremely easy for a new role at another company to be better in a few areas, like comp, while being much less enjoyable for a dozen other reasons. Be careful!

Your manager or company are actually dipshits

Before we get into strategies for dealing with this, it's first worth pointing out that your interpretation of the situation might not be accurate. "Out of touch boss" is pervasive enough to be a cliché and given that many of those "bosses" were promoted up from being a worker just like you, it seems unlikely that so many of them really don't have any idea what the fuck they're doing.

In my experience, this perception is likely tied in part to the fact that the worker may not fully understand their manager's job. It's unlikely that you're getting the full story of what the manager's manager (and organization) expects from them, and what resources they have requested only to have them delayed or denied. And to be fair, the manager may also not be communicating well with you and may be placing weight on the wrong factors related to what really matters to help you do your job.

I say all of that to help you understand that what you're perceiving as "dipshitery" is more likely a combination of constraints, ignorance, competing priorities for their attention, and yes, maybe *some* dipshitery. Understanding this matters because it will help you get into the right mindset to solve the problem.

The best approach in this situation is to postpone worrying about what you're trying to gain for yourself, and instead, have a discussion with your manager that begins by asking them what *they need*. How can *you* help *them* be successful? Everyone should do this on a regular basis, independently of any self-serving agenda. This question and the affect the answers will have on your thinking and prioritization, is the key gate between individual-contributor or a low-level manager, and the next levels up, manager of managers or leadership.

But as an IC seeking recognition, resources, or comp, this is the key that unlocks the gate. It helps you get your head out of the trees-level and up to the forest-level. By understanding the knobs and dials, and most importantly, the critical constraint, success and failure gauges, on your manager's flight console, you can ensure your contributions are totally aligned with green and success, and equally as important, you know how to talk about your work that way, and how what you're asking for aligns directly with those same objectives.

Simple examples:

- Frame the request for a new software utility in terms of how it will *enable you to deliver* critical Q2 goal X on deadline, not in terms of how it will make the team's lives easier.

- For your comp request, use the tips in the section above, and add something like "I can understand I might need another offer to demonstrate that I'm worth what I'm asking for, but it seems stupid for me to waste time on that when we have critical deliverable X. What do you think I should do?"

Keep in mind that OKRs and employee and team goals are not the same thing. Yes, your manager may have explicit, organization-set goals, but here we're looking at a meta-level above that. There are often objectives that didn't get codified into formal goals which would deliver more direct value for your manager. Ask.

Always frame your manager requests as a *partnership*, because it is.

Other Unidentified Constraints, Blockers, and Issues

Assuming your request is reasonable, you may find yourself in a situation where your manager still seems to be dragging their feet. Something to consider is that continued delays could be a sign of a yet-to-be revealed financial stressor on the organization. If you suspect this, rather than talk about it with other employees, ask your manager directly, and make it clear you came to them first with these concerns. Hopefully you'll either get some transparency on a real issue, or if there is no issue, your manager will be motivated to push your request through to avoid fueling any speculation that could create broader problems.

But no, really, what if it's actually dipshits?

If you have problems with your company and/or your manager, the leadership team, your co-workers, any of the myriad components that can make your work experience fundamentally undesirable, you should spend your energy on an exit plan. If you are generally unhappy with your employer, role, etc., getting paid more is a temporary band-aid. I don't recommend you invest time trying to find happiness in a bad situation through comp.

One other thing to consider is that if this happens to you repeatedly, where you change companies or teams and everyone always seems to come up short, the problem is likely at least partly *you*. Whoa, easy there, hold off on throwing the book for a few more seconds.

I've been in situations where my personal life stresses reached a level that affected the self I brought to work. Particularly if those stresses accumulated somewhat gradually, you and the people immediately around you might not see an abrupt enough change to recognize it. Six months or a year of cumulative shit later and you may be unhappy, depressed, anxious, but to you the feeling may seem to be tied to a reflection of your world, vs being severely over-wound inside yourself. It's usually not that difficult to recognize when you're stressed, but what can be really challenging is to recognize *the degree*. You could be a ten while thinking you're a two.

This can be a very hard position to be in, and I'm more qualified to train ballerinas than make mental health recommendations, but if this *might* be you, before you make major life changes seeking a fix, I suggest talking to your family and friends to see what they think about how you're doing and possibly getting some professional help.

You're not living life right if you never make a decision that could possibly lead to major failure and pain, I've done it a few times, but anything is ultimately manageable and survivable. It's the fundamental mechanism that life uses to get you back to 100% so it can fuck with you again by luring you into trying to ride another canyon-jumping rocket. You'll be fine, but get some fucking help.

You Are Wrong

And finally, what may be the most important collaboration advice.

I've worked with people from a lot of countries and cultures. Because I only speak fairly sloppy American English and a smattering of impractical French, when I was in my late 20s, I thought it might be helpful to invest some time in learning some critical phrases in other languages.

After some list making and draconian prioritization, I realized that I could satisfy 80 to 90 percent of my needs by learning one phrase in as many languages as possible.

That phrase is "you are wrong".

I then proceeded to learn how to say "you are wrong" in as many languages as possible. At one point I knew this phrase in something like 20 languages.

Here are some of them using English-phonetic pronunciation, which is the way I remember it, because of my aforementioned language speaking-and-comprehension limitations.

"Toom Galut Ho" is Hindi.

"Tee Nyet Prav" is Russian.

"Nee Tswoah Laaaa" is Mandarin Chinese. Draw that "laaaaaa" out to make it funnier.

I was once in a taxi going from Manhattan to Jersey City, New Jersey at about 2am. I noticed my driver's name printed on his ID card looked similar to one of my co-workers, who was from West Africa, from an area that spoke a language called "Tvi" ("tvee").

We were riding in silence, and I leaned forward and said to the driver, in what I correctly guessed was his native language, that he was wrong. He said "what...?" then started laughing so hard he almost wrecked the car. We had a great chat for the rest of the ride.

If you know a language well enough to use it passably, it's probably a terrible idea to use it to tell a native speaker that they're wrong. However, if you don't speak their language *at all*, but you tell them *you are wrong*, it's a fantastic ice breaker, and you should immediately add that to your networking toolbox.

51

The [Insert F500 Company] Stories

In my life I've had three major-impact stories directly related to me doing tech work for American Express. I'll tell them out of chronological order, #2,#3, then finally #1.

First, some background. I lived in New York during the entire 1990s, with the original goal of being an artist. As I've explained elsewhere in the book, that began with a job at a major publishing company where happenstance introduced me to computers, and between that job and some freelance work, I earned my income doing catalog design for publishing companies until about 1994, when I completed my Master of Fine Arts at Rutgers.

I had another full-time programming job on 57th Street near Madison Avenue in 95-96, and it was a strange place. It was a very small company, owned by a middle-aged guy with significant second-generation wealth.

This was when laptops first came out that were smaller than a suitcase and were actually usable, and this guy made sure he always had the latest and best. I remember the day when his $8,000 IBM arrived, I'm fairly sure a seven pound 760 with probably 30 minutes of battery life, replacing something else that was no more than six months old.

He lived on Park Avenue, maybe ten blocks away, and had a full-time chauffeur. Whenever his wife wanted to mail something, she would call her husband's secretary, let's call her Alice. The wife would tell Alice what to put on the envelope, Alice would type it up and then go down and wait on 57th street for the chauffeur to drive down to pick up the single typed envelope. I absolutely shit you not. I was once summoned along with our CIO to work on the owner's child's computer. Their apartment was quite nice.

The CIO, my direct manager, was a gay Libertarian from Pittsburg who looked like a more-handsome Dolph Lundgren. We'll call him Gary. Gary and I worked in the same room and had many splendid arguments about privatized fire departments and personal sovereignty. A year prior, Gary had informed the Internal Revenue Service that his sovereign status meant that they had no legal authority for taxation, and therefore he would not be paying them again. He also demanded, in what in hindsight might have arguably been a step too far, that they immediately refund all of his previous payments.

Gary was a good programmer and an even better creative thinker when it came to one-level-higher software design. The first project I worked on there was a system he had built that had a ton of CRUD forms, and he had realized very early that his job could become a miserable grind of programming and maintaining each of these screens. So instead, he had the brilliant idea of programming a settings-driven rendering engine that could generate the form code at runtime from rows of configuration properties stored in a table within the application database. To create a new form, he just added the settings and it worked with no coding. My god was this so much better! This was my first exposure to a practical example of coding to generate code, and it forever changed how I thought about programming.

I used a variation of the same model a few years later for an Amex project. In my 1999 version, it could generate a fully working CRUD HTML form for any SQL table, and my team was able to build complete applications in a couple of days. It was a massive difference maker, yet more than two decades later I still don't see this as a normalized practice, while people are still writing an absolute fuck-ton of set-left-equal-to-right object-oriented horseshit code. It boggles my mind.

Last I heard, Gary was being hunted by, and actively hiding from, agents of the IRS, but hopefully he sorted that out, and if not, I'm sure he'll be getting out soon.

The final strange moment happened after I'd been there for a few months. They hired a finance person, a young woman, and one day I was doing an update to her computer, and I noticed her name written on a piece of paper at her desk. I had been introduced to her, and there were only 6 or 7 people in the office, but somehow I didn't understand her last name until I saw it written down. Basquiat. "Do you know the painter", I said.

"He was my brother." We had more conversations about that, and I went to her wedding and visited her apartment, which was a standard Queens apartment for a late-20s accountant in 1995, except for the Basquiat paintings on the wall. As someone who just completed an art degree, and was doing Windows upgrades in that wacky office, it was a strange connection indeed.

I left there to make art and bounced between more freelance coding work to pay the bills. Finally, on an unusually high debt cycle, I thought "I should probably focus on making some money", and in 1998 I took a consultant-programmer role with American Express.

Amex Story 2: Career Humility

Starting in 2000, I began working on a custom business intelligence platform to provide analytics and reporting for the Merchant group in American Express. They've re-organized a few times, but the two big divisions in the credit card business are the cardmember side, and the merchants-who-accept-the-card side.

I describe the database tech for that era in another part of the book, but the app was an Active Server Pages (ASP, pre-.NET) web site, which I coded in VBScript using only Windows notepad (not notepad++). If you've written a significant app in a non-code-aware text editor, give me a sign when we meet and I'll lean in for a hug with back-thump because we both know. For y'all that have only ever coded with syntax highlighting, code completion, and now Co-Pilot and GPT, I agree we should use the best tools at our disposal, but I'll still stare you straight in the eyes and blow smoke off the barrels of my notepad-coding finger-guns all. fucking. day. Until one of those OG punch card warriors walks up, then we can both give them a deep bow.

The ASP site connected directly to a SQL Server database, and as I mentioned above, all the CRUD forms were rendered by interpreting settings from application definition tables stored in the database. Even better, all of the HTML was generated within stored procedures. See if you can wrap your head around this: yes, the VBScript in ASP opened a database connection, ran a proc, and sent whatever came back to the browser. *Of course* it only worked on Internet Explorer, Todd.

In addition to the ability to support very rapid creation of new analytics screens, this app had a couple bits of special sauce that we ultimately patented. Amex is the patent owner, and I'm the primary inventor.

As time passed and the app matured, it became a true multi-function "operating system". We eventually added a Sales CRM capability and a dozen other minor utility apps. It was going great, with the only downside being that the total development costs were steadily rising.

Here's an aside with two important tips. A lot of great applications start as unofficial skunkworks projects run directly by the business users, outside of a formal technology organization. Overall, I think this can be a good thing, and should happen more often, as high-powered tech continues to get easier to use, and no-code, low-code solutions get better and better. However, if those projects become wildly successful, there may be significant risk of them being damaged in a battle for ownership, like two gorillas trying to hold an orchid at the same time.

The second problem is a side-effect of the "operating system"-type application. Often these start as a simple single function app, but if the team is good and fast, and the quality of the app is high, before long everyone with shitty apps or good ideas will come knocking at your door to have you incorporate that functionality in your super-app. There's nothing wrong with that, and I think it can be great and high-ROI for the business.

However, the problem with this is that as the costs migrate from a bunch of different small initiatives to the budget line for your do-everything-app, someone high above in the executive leadership zeppelin's caviar lounge is going to see it, spit out their champagne, and exclaim "what the fuck is this?" I want to make sure this is clear for people who haven't experienced this before. Consolidation is great, and invariably leads to a reduction in *total costs*. However, consolidation may take a bunch of apps and systems that cost $2 million a year, but split up into a bunch of less visible smaller budgets, and turn them into a single, better system that costs $1 million a year, which *shows up on a single line of a spreadsheet*. Every time I've been involved in a successful consolidation project, this same dynamic happens.

Much like every band who owe a debt to heroin for profound early career success, a technology project that has matured enough to be radar-targeted by both finance and the formal tech org had best recognize that it's time to make some changes.

Because, if you're still reading this, you likely think of me as a not-entirely-dipshit, as you anticipate, I was all the fuck over this. My proposal to reduce the cost for Amex while protecting the project (for them) and my team and my bank account (for me), was to enter into a formal license agreement wherein my company would be permitted to sell the generally applicable functionalities of the platform to other companies, in return for free updates of the core product for Amex. My business stakeholders, because they understood success, math, and money, loved it.

Around this time, as though God stood up to take a leak and refresh his scotch leaving no one to hold the karma-destiny steering wheel for a minute, there was a slight leadership re-org, and we got a new VP project-owner. So that we don't foreshadow the rest of the story, let's pick a neutral name and call him Bob. Robert F. Shithead.

Bob Shithead, who I later learned was also a pig with his female subordinates, played the gregarious host during our meetings in his office. During one of our conversations over a still-warm print-out of one of our licensing agreement drafts, Bob volunteered, and here I quote verbatim, "I make a lot of money". This would be a totally normal thing for him to have said, if in fact he was having a stroke, which he was not.

"We agree in principle", he said, after a fourth or fifth draft came back from the Amex general counsel with even more egregiously them-favorable terms (for example, we would never own our own future extensions to the licensed IP). And like the complete fucking optimistic dumbass I was born to be, the months passed, and we kept shoveling-in more intellectual property, connecting it to our existing work-for-hire consulting terms and thereby making it inaccessible to us if our agreement didn't come through.

Another consequence of Bob's incompetence beyond how it impacted us, was that it was visible to his superiors. Eventually they made the wise decision to chuck Bob like the useless ballast that he was, which put our project and our relationship with the company in play. Which is when the concern I helpfully predicted above, regarding the formal tech org's interest in killing or absorbing any business skunkworks that was successful, sprang forth in the form of a woman we'll call Karen, a tech-org VP into whose lap our homeless project suddenly fell.

After many more months of discussion, in early December 2003, Karen summoned my business partner and I, another developer on the project team who had founded the company with me, to Phoenix for the stated purpose of finalizing the details of our licensing agreement.

Some additional context. By this time, I had moved back to Ohio, and I had a small consulting company that was doing most of the development on this project with Amex. My business partners included two great people, both had been programmers with me at Amex in New York. Things were going well, but everything hinged on the successful outcome of the Amex licensing agreement. At that point, my first child was about three months old, and had not slept yet.

We entered a conference room in Phoenix at 9am on probably a Tuesday at the beginning of December. Karen was seated at the end of the table, and within 5 minutes of us sitting down, she gestured to two Indian men sitting in chairs on the side of the room and introduced them as the people we would immediately begin training to take over our project. As in, beginning to train them for the three days we'd planned to be in Phoenix to finish the licensing agreement, starting right that instant. Yes, that was every bit as fucked up as it sounds. We stood up, walked out, and flew home.

Everyone should spend 99% of their time being very nice. I am an antagonistically-inclined human, so it is only deep breaths and humor that makes me remotely tolerable. I frequently imagine a moment, a hundred thousand years from now, when I appear magically on a clifftop somewhere in the universe, with one other random human. After conversation we discover that we both lived not only on Earth, but in the U.S. at the end of the 20th century. I don't care who that fucker is, we're going to hug and laugh and share a shit ton of remember-that-time stories, as two people with no more commonality than being on the same side of this rock at about the same time. And I consider anyone I *actually know*, to be way more connected with me than that.

So be nice. But also, when it is inarguably and emphatically necessary, be able to tell everyone to go fuck themselves and proceed to burn it all down.

Back home the next day, our business stakeholders from New York were calling. "You can't just leave", they said. "I most certainly can", I replied, reminding everyone that in the absence of the agreement we were working on, any of them or us could walk away at any time. "What do you need", they said.

The licensing agreement was over, the project would certainly get transitioned away from us... what did I need? Two things: guaranteed billing for my full team for four more months, and the transition had to be covered by a new contract, under a new Master Consulting Agreement that made us an approved American Express vendor.

Another pro tip: in any big company, navigating the procurement process is the sales equivalent of an Everest summit. When I first started working with Amex, the procurement process was lean and kind of insane. Any employee of a reasonable authority level, Director or above, could form contracts for services with basically anyone. This was pretty normal before the Y2K tech-investment hangover, which allowed me to get in as a literal nobody and have a basic contract. However, after Y2K, as finance reviewed their tech and consulting expenditures like someone who wakes up in a wine-filled body bag might review their prior night, the downsides of those decisions were clear, and everything got way the fuck tighter.

In December 2003, there were no more than four total companies on the American Express global vendor list for technology services. IBM, Accenture, Tata, and Infosys. I said, "My team and I will stay until April 1 if you put our company of eight employees on that list." So they did.

We invested in the transition of our "baby", the project we thought we were going to raise to adulthood, to the new offshore team. Our team members that we couldn't keep all found jobs during that four-month window, and when we finished out the transition, I sent three bottles of Dom Perignon to the Phoenix office and asked them to take good care of our app.

Six months later, when I was back on the Amex network for another project, I took a look at our old app. On an app that previously had daily deployments, there had been no code changes since we left. Zero. There would be no more changes, and the app was sunset out a couple of years later. The transition killed something that could have delivered a lot more value to both Amex and us.

Around that same time, as we struggled to keep our business alive and pull the plane back up above the treetops, out of nowhere, one afternoon I got a call from none other than our old friend Bob Shithead. He told me he was looking for work and asked if I had anything. Yes, he had some basic competency problems, but understood our history well enough that it was obvious his call was an act of desperation. It really hit me, and I've thought about it many times since. Whether they've realized it or not, in no small part because of that call, I've always looked at anyone who's worked for me or reported to me as someone I might be working *for* someday. No kidding, I mean *every* person I've worked with.

But humble or not, of course I didn't hire Bob Motherfucking Shithead.

A few years later when my next business had collapsed and my marriage was officially over, my brothers and I did a post-divorce bachelor party trip to Las Vegas. While I don't feel it was pronounced enough to be an official "chip on my shoulder", the unrelated negative aftermath of those other life events made me a bit reflective on the theme of them-that-done-me-wrong. In this spirit, to memorialize my feelings about the episode described here, I got the two Amex patent numbers tattooed on my ass.

A few more years later, I was contacted by an American Express lawyer about those same patents, which it seemed were the best chance Amex had in a countersuit for a lawsuit filed against one of their recent-acquisition subsidiaries. Would I be willing to be deposed? Certainly!

I spent a day answering questions under oath about the tech and the invention history of the patents. I had come there with the singular goal of referencing the patent numbers being on my ass, and thus having a discussion about my ass entered into the official record. It was the long-play joke and right-parenthesis that this story needed. But alas, I failed you good people. So far.

Amex Story 3: Bigger

In August of 2005, I got a random call from a friend, a former colleague at Amex, who was still at Amex. I was at home hanging out with my son, who was now two and insane.

Me: "Hey man, what's up?"

Him: "I've got a question." [proceeds to describe a complex banking transaction system] "How long do you think it should take to build something like that?"

Me: "Six months maybe."

I hear harumphs and hubbub on his end. I realize he's cold-called me from a conference room full of people, and I'm on speaker phone.

Him: "So doable by the end of the year?"

Me: "It's a lot of work, but sure."

Him: "Fantastic." And he hung up.

A few hours later, I emailed him and said, "that thing you asked me about... we could build it."

He called me the next day, and we were off to the races.

I want to take a moment for an advice aside. I've been in this position many times now, where someone describes a really challenging objective, and asks you if you can do it. Every single time, these moments have been pivotal for me. In 2005, our company had survived with five of us: two great developers and three partners. We were still primarily working for American Express, leveraging our Master Consulting Agreement and approved vendor status to get work from other parts of the company. But it was far from stable... we were using the revenue to pay the two developers, but the two other partners and I were largely surviving on our own savings. I burned through my IRA and investment account and was coming down to fumes.

When you get a call from someone you trust, who trusts you, who is trying to accomplish something amazing and extends an invitation to go along with them on that ride, and they ask you if it can be done, that's a unique kind of moment. Your answer will likely impact a number of lives, and the journey will certainly be all-in difficult. Maybe rewarding, maybe devastating, maybe both.

I know what it means to answer a question like that, and my answer has always been "yes". That I ever had a team that would trust me to grab one parachute and throw us all out of the plane is one of the most humbling experiences of my life, and I'm very grateful.

What happened next was crazy.

We had a hard deadline of January 1, 2006. The product we were working on was a health savings account (HSA) connected to an Amex credit card. Because it was connected to a health insurance enrollment period, there was zero tolerance for delivering late, which is why our ability to confidently say "yes" beat out the incumbent alternative, our old nemesis, the internal American Express technology organization, who said it couldn't be done.

The Fall of 2005 was bananas. We were hiring as fast as possible, coding like lunatics, and dealing with the fucks from the Amex tech org who were sour-grapes auditing the shit out of us. I want to underscore that last point. Theoretically, we were "same team". The deadline of Jan 1 that we were able to say yes to, was an absolutely hard date upon which the viability of this project depended. The fact that we were able to commit to this and attempting to deliver at what turned out to be great pain and suffering, should have been a moment of support and collaboration. But no. These motherfuckers came out to Ohio multiple times, with the objectives of telling us we couldn't possibly do this, and attempting to ensure we couldn't do this with assassination-level security audits.

I remember one exchange, with one of the Amex tech VPs in our office, who started by asking if the area was going through a downturn. We're in a good community. It's not the fucking Hamptons or Bel Air, but by any reasonable measure it's great. "It looks a little rough here... is the economy struggling?"

"Ha, ha, go fuck yourself, Brian."

He then said, "you can't possibly get all of this done in the next three months". To which I replied, "could your team get this done in the next three months?" The correct answer to that question was "no, of course my team couldn't get this done", but I knew this fuck could neither admit to that, nor dare risk that if he said "yes", the business team calls his bluff and brings the project back in-house, committed to deliver by year-end. His reply was a five-minute words-and-hand-gestures recreation of the Homer Simpson fades-into-bushes meme.

We also set up a new office, in a floor of a building that hadn't had tenants for decades, and for some reason the heat was hit or miss in the office that year. I distinctly remember 3am nights coding with fingers so cold it hurt to type. We met our deadline, and it was absolutely glorious.

In 2006, we kept hiring and working like machines. I met some of my favorite people, including Don Boscoe and others I still keep in touch with today. There were many hilarious days and hilarious nights. By the end of the year, our Amex executive stakeholders were organizing a spin-off of this new product to its own company, and talking about an acquisition of our company to act as the technology organization for this new entity. I never burned a hundred-dollar bill, but I ended the year dancing quietly in a bathroom like I imagine people capable of burning hundred-dollar bills just might.

2007 was different. The health care card we were supporting was a proof-of-concept, and there were two basic obstacles to its viability. First, it relied on the card being accepted for payment at a doctor or hospital at the time of service. We had some great secret sauce technology that could park a card-swipe pre-authorization much longer than normal, and then match the point-of-sale card swipe to one or more adjudicated health insurance claims that would come in much later. The idea was to make an HSA extremely easy to use by allowing you to fund your out-of-pocket expenses via a line of credit if you didn't have savings, but seamlessly use savings if you had some. This was not easy to do, but making this work was a great experience for the customer, and our whole team, about 35 people, had become the second company to wholly adopt the new product, right after Amex itself. But at that point, only a small percentage of doctors and hospitals accepted American Express.

The second thing that this product relied on was that the United States health care marketplace stayed the same.

In 2007, a young idealist named Barack Obama decided to run for President. On his list of shit to tackle was the appalling state of U.S. healthcare and private sector insurance. He wasn't wrong, but fuuuuuck.

By April of 2007, we were holding more than a million dollars of already-earned billing for work done by our team in the first three months of the year, waiting for our budgets to be approved. I went to New York and had a meeting in an American Express board room with a Senior Vice President and said, "I need my million dollars now". Think about that for a minute.

The faucet opened and I got our million dollars, but a few months later, in June, I got the dreaded bad news phone call. The project had been cancelled because the Amex acceptance rate for health care providers was too low, and they estimated it would take something like a fifty million dollar a year marketing investment for the next five years to close that gap enough to have the health card make sense. And this would be happening against a political backdrop that might fundamentally change the health insurance industry and potentially make the product unviable. This had nothing to do with our work, we had fucking crushed it, but these other external obstacles killed it.

A few days later, I hosted a company all-hands at a small movie theater just down the street from our office, where we'd recently started to do some morning meetings, because at thirty-nine employees, we were too big for any room in the office. I sat on a stage at the theater and explained what was going on. After that, we went back to the office, and I personally fired 22 people, one at a time, one after another, until it was done.

I have had to do a bulk layoff twice, and both times I told everyone personally, one on one. This is in addition to the time in story #3, when I had to let people go, but I was able to give them four months' notice.

Up to and during those years, and for a long time after, I kept two framed New York Times articles on my office wall. They were both profiles of Ken Chenault, who was the future-CEO-anointed, then CEO, of American Express from shortly after I started in 1998 (formal in 2001), until after I was gone, in 2017. One of the articles was just after 9/11, when they lost employees in the Trade Center, the sudden halt to travel was killing their business, and their headquarters building was unusable because a fucking terrorist attack collapsed the building across the street, which hit Amex HQ on the way down. The article included a picture of Mr. Chenault, looking grim but with eyes that said, "I got this".

The second article was a puff piece from a few years later. American Express was doing great, and this time the picture put Ken standing, arm on a chairback, looking confident as all fuck, as if to say, "told you so motherfuckers".

For those scoring at home, yes, this was the second time I boarded the World Series game seven bus with American Express and woke up naked and barely alive in a New Jersey chemical run-off swamp. Except this time, the blast radius was much larger, affecting the team we had created, many people I cared about, and my long relationship with my business partners. And yes, as you might anticipate, though I had at that point never met my future wife, the twenty-two I fired that day did include she who would be my future sister-in-law, because about every five years God loses patience and tries to see if he can beat the level in the sim-game of my life by just mashing fucking buttons.

[Fourth wall break: my sister-in-law, Abby, was one of my draft readers, and her note on the prior paragraph was *"I made it into the book!* <some emoji the kids use>". She's a big deal VP now, and I still feel bad about firing her. At the first family Christmas her sister brought me to, where I was under-dressed and had a pronounced black eye, the first question their mom asked me was why I fired her daughter. My life is a lot like a ballet performance where the lead is a three-year-old wearing pants made out of inflated balloons, and there's no music. It's basically a four-hour seizure accompanied by the sound of squeeking whenever his thighs touch. For the audience, it's highly uncomfortable, but the kid seems to be having a great time.]

Amex Story 1: Life and Death

Before the stories above, other things happened, which in hindsight are kind of fantastical (not "fantastic"... definitely not fantastic). I never made this connection until the moment when I'm typing this sentence, but...

My favorite author is Kurt Vonnegut. I won't hold-forth at length here, the best advice is to just read all of his novels. Slaughterhouse Five remains to this day the only book I've ever sat down and read cover-to-cover without standing up.

The connective spine of Slaughterhouse Five is both a narrative device and what we read as the true experience of the main character, Billy Pilgrim, that he has become "unstuck in time". His consciousness continually bounces between different periods of his life, leaving him in a state of disconnection from every current moment, like he's an observer through his own eyes, and not a participant. One of those periods includes being a prisoner of war in Dresden Germany before and during the Allied firebombing campaign in February of 1945. I haven't found a more apt and beautiful way of describing the experience of post-trauma, and specifically the wall between your ability to internally comprehend and process, and your ability to outwardly explain what you're thinking and feeling. It's like trying to tell a story when you can't find the words for a proper start and end.

My first two years at Amex I was just doing custom reporting. I sat in a 14 by 14 foot windowless beige room on the 35th floor of the Amex tower, at 200 Vesey street in lower Manhattan. Everything about the room was beige. Beige with the vivid filter all the way up. Vivid fucking beige. I encountered those same tan colors in other offices in downtown Manhattan. It's the color of white surfaces after being touched by ten thousand human hands. Colors from a section of the spectrum notable only for its ability to trigger calm and/or despair.

I was in there with three other men, a Chinese guy named Jim who was a little older than me, a Jewish man named Chaim who was about 50, and Tom, who was about 60. Chaim called himself "Charles" at work, his logic being to make it easier for everyone else.

Tom was also ethnically Jewish but had become something of a science-driven agnostic. Both Charles and Tom had parents with concentration camp tattoos. That room was a cauldron.

Further, American Express was in the process of a floor-by-floor remodel, in which they were stripping down to the concrete and rebuilding a new layout on each floor. Generally, the changes made sense. They were eliminating all the offices that were on the perimeter of the floor, because they blocked the views and sunlight for all but the lucky few. These were replaced with three or four rows of cubicles starting at the windows, and the private offices were on the inside. However, the interior shared-space rooms, like we were in, were being consolidated into fewer larger windowless rooms. The design was nicer, except we were going to go from being four in a room, to being twenty or more. Oh, the cacophony! Oh, the smells!

I recognized an opportunity with our weird windowless man-room and the transitional moment we were in. To try to maintain a connection to my art but recognizing my need to be tethered to this job, I decided to embrace the spirit of "love the one you're with", and attempt to make a video documentary of the four of us in our room.

In 1999, the state of "prosumer" video was hi-8 video tape. These were smaller tapes with smaller cameras than Betamax, VHS, or professional systems, but it was still video tape. At the same time, computers were just to the point where a high-end home computer could digitize and enable video editing. Disillusioned with the logistics of creating, moving, and storing large sculpture, I saw the potential for me to use my odd combination of art and tech skills to take advantage of the newly accessible video medium as a new way for me to explore creative ideas. Ironically, it was that project, which evolved into a long-term hobbyist interest in video, that ultimately led to the Old Coder Guy TikTok, which inspired this book.

Sometime in 1999, after getting permission from Chaim, Tom, and Jim, I brought a small video camera to the office, set it up on a tripod and began recording. Over the next three weeks, I recorded about forty hours of candid video, and another four hours of one-on-one interviews. I started recording, and as people visited our room, including our managers, I explained what I was doing, and no one ever asked me to stop. I said that underwhelmingly, but really think about this. I openly filmed an almost 50-hour documentary at my programming job, with a camera the size of a football, and it was just fine.

To enable me to edit on my 486 Windows 95 machine, I bought an external 100GB SCSI RAID array, for something like $1,200. The thing was the size of a tall shoebox and leveraged the advantages of striping content across multiple disks (yes, spinning platter disks) to accelerate I/O enough to enable something as resource intensive as real time video editing. I'm using words, like "computer" and "editing" that still seem to have meaning in the context of modern video processing, but that's about as accurate as assuming both I and the North Sentinel Islanders mean the same thing when we use the words "please don't drop by".

In hindsight I might have entered the game too early. Everything took fucking forever. The tapes needed to be individually digitized, which involved playing the whole tape to be digitally re-recorded into the computer. But to make it worse, at that point, Windows 95 had a 32-bit file system with a maximum single file size of 2GB, and digitizing a one-hour tape would create about 3GB of data, and when it exceeded the 2GB, the app would suddenly die and you'd lose the recording. This meant I had to monitor the process and stop it before it hit the number of minutes that yielded about 2GB.

And even worse than that, all of the video couldn't fit on the RAID array. In fact, in total, it was something like 500GB, and to manage this, I had to backup and restore different sections of video from backup tapes. The amount of time and effort it took just to get to the point where you were trimming video is almost impossible to imagine now.

I was using Adobe Premicre at the time, and if I edited for more than a half an hour and didn't close and re-open the app, it would crash and I'd lose the last unsaved batch of edits, forcing me to have to re-watch and re-cut. Jumping between points in the video might trigger a screen repaint that took 20 to 30 seconds.

Because all of the video couldn't fit on the computer at the same time, I had to use this iterative trimming process, where I edited a couple hours down to ten or so minutes of "candidate clips". I then had Premiere save the project for that section as post-trimmed video files (so keeping just the sections from the source video that were on my rough-edited Premiere timeline), and then backed that up, deleted it, restored another two hours of raw video and repeated the process. Only after months of this, to reduce the original video down to a manageable amount of data, did I return to the first edited projects and start to combine them, repeating the pan-for-gold process again. Given that this was open-ended documentary footage, the logistical challenges and the long time lags it created, which could be six or more months, between seeing the different sections of video, made it extremely difficult to have enough in my head at one time to find the thematic core and the story.

I've revisited that project in my mind many times reflecting on the serendipity of right-place, right-time. For both audio and video production, the years I've been alive have paralleled a truly transformative technology evolution. From incredibly difficult for a low-budget hobbyist, to doable, to easy to do, to easy to do well. For a creator, or potential creator, it's hard to overstate the significance of these changes. There were brilliant people who were not connected to any means of recording and distributing their content. There were other people with means, who spent a huge amount of their available time dealing with the arduousness of pre-digital recording, editing, and distribution, instead of creating. And now those obstacles have been removed and the mechanics of production are getting nearer and nearer to zero friction. Open an app, hit record, and post.

In 2000, however, this took absolutely. fucking. forever.

I finally got to what I thought was a decent "done" version of the video in late 2000, and then some changes happened at my Amex job. Tom and Jim left, and I started working on the project that would become story #2 above, and then later, in 2001, I began making plans to move out of my art warehouse in Jersey City, back to Ohio. The documentary collected dust.

After the move to Ohio in the summer of 2001, I kept the Jersey City space so that I would have a place to stay when I was in New York. Given that this was when remote work was barely possible, let alone normalized, I arranged to alternate two weeks in New York and two weeks in Ohio.

Returning in August, the move had made it real, and I recognized that regardless of the near-term plan, my time in New York was coming to a close. I arranged with Chaim, who was still at Amex, to reserve a conference room after work one day during my next planned trip, and contacted Tom and Jim and invited them to join us for the first-ever screening of the movie. I hadn't seen either of those guys in at least a year, so we were all excited to get together, and I was beyond thrilled to be bringing the creation part of this long project to an end, with the goal of sharing it more broadly soon after.

The morning of our screening, I put a digital video camera containing the tape of the single final edit of "Room" (the name of the documentary... what else could you call it?) and a couple of charged batteries in my backpack and headed to the ferry to go to work.

That was Tuesday, September 11, 2001.

September 11, 2001

The next morning started out normally, taking the World Financial Center ferry from Jersey City, and walking past the WFC marina on a beautiful, clear, sunny early-Fall morning. I went inside the Amex building, went to the cafeteria to get coffee, and that was when the first plane hit. As I left the cafeteria, the security people were already directing everyone out of the building.

Outside, I went around the corner from Vesey to the West Side Highway, to get a better look at what was going on. The street was already filling with NYPD and NYFD, setting up barricades and keeping people back, but I was allowed to stay where I was, which was directly across the street from the burning North tower. At that moment, what we thought we were seeing was the result of an awful accident. I remember sipping coffee and holding a banana in the other hand, looking straight up at that giant building burning, with all the firefighters running around like ants in the street below, thinking "how the hell are they going to put that out".

And then there was the sound of a large jet flying way too low, and I looked right and watched it bank into the side of the south tower and explode through the building. And now I was watching two burning skyscrapers, and the whole world had changed.

This was my exact position: 40.71372, -74.01433.

To understand what my brain did in that moment, you only need to appreciate one key detail. When the first building was burning, I was watching an accident. When the second building was hit, it instantly transformed undebatably into an intentional attack. I've never experienced this another time in my life, but it was like a circuit breaker tripped in my brain, and for the next thirty minutes, I became an emotionless machine. Unstuck in time, if you will.

The police immediately pushed us to get out of the neighborhood, toward the Hudson River or move uptown. I turned the corner to head West on Vesey, and I was suddenly surrounded by people who hadn't seen the second plane because our building was in the way.

Try to picture this. These people are on an unplanned hiatus from the start of their workday. They're smoking and shooting the shit and are oblivious to what's going on 20 steps away around the corner. They could not see the first building burning, and they had no idea yet about the second plane. I felt like a time traveller from a few minutes in the future. I consciously thought to myself, well they'll know soon enough, and what would I even say? As I mechanically walked to the ferry that would take me back across the river to my warehouse in New Jersey, I dropped my coffee and banana in a trash can, and as I did it, I remember my arms looked like arms on a video game screen, like I was standing behind myself.

At no time did it occur to me that I had a ready-to-go video camera in my backpack. I didn't think this consciously, but I had mentally registered that the camera and tape (the only tape I had with me) was for something else, something important. It didn't at all occur to me then that the other objective was now irrelevant and impossible. Not for a second did I consider taking my camera out. I was on a side of the event from which I've seen almost no video, it would have been a unique additional perspective.

This was something I regretted for a long time, but now I'm glad I didn't take out the camera. Once filming, I wouldn't have left. I would have watched and recorded increasingly horrific things. Likely created another source for people to scan looking for last sightings of loved ones, and probably made another set of jumpers famous for the worst moment, what should be the least-defining moment, of their lives.

This is where I was when the buildings fell: 40.72042, -74.03701. I stuck my head out of the window of the fifth floor of my warehouse and watched them go down in a cloud.

I went out in the evening, probably six or seven, and I stopped at the ferry terminal, which was just at the end of my block. I have some video of this, which includes a silent crowd watching a ferry arriving and unloading people who are clearly in shock. In the background is a giant plume of smoke from the trade center site, illuminated by the sunset behind me.

One of the towers had a giant cell antenna on top, so when the buildings fell, it fucked up cell service for a good part of Manhattan, Brooklyn, and Jersey City. After about 10am my phone had no service, and I spent the rest of the day completely alone. As I walked away from the ferry terminal and along the road by the river to go find some dinner, my phone rang, and it was my friend, former co-worker, and client-server SQL mentor, Scott Jerome-Parks, just calling to see if I was ok. It might have been the best single phone call of my life.

The You've-Got-to-Be-Fucking-Kidding-Me Saga of Scott Jerome-Parks

Scott was a senior Sybase DBA and Unix admin consultant who had started working with Amex in 1999 or so. He was brought in as part of an upgrade process to move us off of the file-based database solutions, like FoxPro, dBase, Access, that we were using for large data applications. He was hired right after a Gandalf-meets-Jerry-Garcia Unix guy whose first activity was to stand up two servers, which would go on to host the core merchant and prospect analytics platform for the next decade, that he, of course, named Cartman and Kenny. Yes, I learned client-server SQL on a half-million-dollar Sybase server named Cartman. [Chef's kiss, God].

This is going to sound like some sort of insult, but I truly don't intend it to be. I'm just painting a picture and trying to do it as honestly as possible. Scott always reminded me of Dilbert. Not the comic strip, I mean the actual character. He looked like Dilbert.

Further, he was a great fucking guy, smart as hell, trying to be helpful, provide mentoring support to a bunch of dipshits, and good advice to the company, at the same time he had fuckwits irreversibly naming expensive critical servers after South Park characters. He was the optimistic competent protagonist surrounded by knuckleheads. Like Dilbert.

In September 2001, Scott had recently left Amex and was working for a different company that was also next to the trade center, in one of the buildings on the south edge of the trade center site that was partially damaged in the attack. For those that may not remember, there were three types of damaged buildings on 9/11; those that were totally destroyed, those that were severely damaged but didn't fall down and needed demolition later, and those that were damaged but later repaired.

The Amex building was one of the latter. It was grazed when the North tower collapsed, but not structurally damaged. One funny thing, before 9/11 Amex operated a data center on the fourth floor of their building, and among other things, it housed the Lotus Notes email servers for New York and most of the east coast, as well as servers supporting business applications, including the ones I was working on. Due to the damage to the building, which knocked the corner off the fourth floor and opened the data center to all of the dust, the servers were toast. The email servers had daily tape backup, with one of the daily backups going offsite each week, let's say that was Sunday or Monday's backup. In theory, the offsite backup could have been as "fresh" as Monday, September 10, one day before. Except the latest box of tapes for offsite hadn't gone out and were sitting on a table in the datacenter on the morning of 9/11... and were also totally fucked. They lost just over a week of communication history.

I had driven to New York from Ohio two days before, on Sunday the ninth, so I wasn't affected by any of the plane groundings or flight restrictions after 9/11. I stayed in New York until Thursday morning, after we had reconvened using phone trees and I confirmed I couldn't help in NY. I arrived home to Ohio Thursday night, September 13th, and by the next day, my team was already talking about me going to Phoenix.

The primary Amex data center at the time was in Phoenix Arizona. The plan was to ship the most recent viable backups for all the New York servers to Phoenix and stand them all up as-was (same names, same everything) in the Phoenix data center. The concern in New York, though, was that with the volume of systems impacted, that process was going to be chaotic bordering on insane. By that point, I had developed a reputation for being a person who could "figure it out", and given that I was already 20% of the way across the country, it was a no-brainer. A few days after 9/11, I drove across the country to Phoenix.

The round trip was about a week, and I drove the thirty hours each way straight, stopping only for one 6-hour night in a motel. I had to pull over to join "war room" calls from places where I had decent cell signal, and I still remember joining a call on the way out at about 8pm from the West side of St. Louis, sitting in the car in the dark and rain.

My motivation to do this was that the team that I'd worked with every day for a few years were sitting in their homes in and around New York, with no ability to communicate with their work colleagues, no office to go to, no ability to distract themselves with normal habits to take their minds off of the incredibly shitty realities of what this meant for their world, our country, and their city. My brother, who at that time lived in Manhattan below 14th street, couldn't go back to his apartment for a while. He worked for a rigging company that did work for the stock exchange, and he has a picture of himself in a bucket-lift hanging the American flag on the front of the New York stock exchange building just a couple days later, in a mask, with the empty neighborhood under an inch of dust below him. With no ability to help with the core problem (the rescue operation at the massive smoking hole in the ground), everyone found other means to contribute, and a little positivity and hope goes a long way.

Which brings us back to Scott, who we left with a new job in an inaccessible building, and a tremendously kind heart. Because he couldn't work due to his damaged office, he decided to volunteer at ground zero. He did support work for the NYFD, NYPD, and the other emergency services who were conducting search and recovery efforts at the site. Nothing more glamorous than making sure they had water.

A few years later, Scott developed a form of tongue cancer that never happens to non-drinking, non-smokers of Scott's age. At that point, the main concern was how much of his tongue he would lose, and how much it would affect eating and speech. And then he went for radiation treatment.

From a New York Times story that appeared on January 24, 2010:

"On the morning of March 14 [2005], Ms. Kalach revised Mr. Jerome-Parks's treatment plan using Varian software. Then, with the patient waiting in the wings, a problem arose, state records show.

Shortly after 11 a.m., as Ms. Kalach was trying to save her work, the computer began seizing up, displaying an error message. The hospital would later say that similar system crashes 'are not uncommon with the Varian software, and these issues have been communicated to Varian on numerous occasions.'

An error message asked Ms. Kalach if she wanted to save her changes before the program aborted. She answered yes. At 12:24 p.m., Dr. Berson approved the new plan.

At 12:57 p.m., six minutes after yet another computer crash, the first of several radioactive beams was turned on."

And then they lit him up.

If you are a technologist working on critical life-and-death systems, I hope you take this story to heart. I'm pretty sure that if Scott, as a programmer, had known about the above problems, he would have requested a detailed root cause analysis, and not said "well, if it worked after you rebooted it, I'm cool to proceed".

People who saw Scott later that day and the next made statements like "Please believe me. His face is so blown up. It's dreadful. There is something wrong", and despite this, they hit him two more times.

To irradiate the back of the tongue, the beam must pass through the upper spinal cord and the brain stem. After realizing the errors and halting treatment, in the following few days, the doctors explained to Scott and his wife that the amount of radiation he had received, where he had received it, would kill him. Based on how the time went, I think it's fair to use the word 'unfortunately', it took two years to finish the job.

One of my business partners, who was another programmer and friend of Scott, from our days together in an Amex contractor room, went with me to see him in the hospital when it was getting near the end. Scott's grace in that situation was hard to comprehend and I won't describe that visit here.

Scott passed away in March of 2007 at the age of 43. I think he would have liked this book, but definitely not this part. Likely his least fucking favorite chapter of any book ever written. He also would have challenged my decision to use so much profanity, and that's just one of the many ways his untimely death left us, and by us, I mean "humanity", with a less-great world.

Another irony: Scott was the first person to show me this new thing called "Google". In hindsight he may have been making the very first "let me Google that for you" joke, as a polite way of telling me to stop interrupting him with Unix questions. And now his life is summarized by a Google-legacy about his death. Searching "Scott Jerome-Parks" returns pages of medical radiation fail stories. Read them anytime you have too much happiness and you want to knock it back down by 80+%.

Aftermath

The collapse of the towers directly affected a very large area, the footprint of the World Trade Center and the immediately surrounding buildings. But the collateral consequences for all of downtown were significant and immediate. By eliminating so much office space, one of the most commuted-to work districts on the planet became a ghost town overnight. If you had a restaurant or any other kind of store, you were faced with at least a few weeks of total closure, and then, if you re-opened, you would have far fewer customers. The Trade Center had included a large subway station, serving multiple NYC train lines, and the Path train to New Jersey, which was destroyed, making the surrounding neighborhood even more logistically isolated.

Because of the geography of the World Financial Center, which is the collection of office buildings on the western edge of the island immediately adjacent to the Trade Center, most of its access to the rest of the city was cut off due to the damage next door. The American Express building was in the Financial Center, on the corner directly across the street from the North tower, and it had some minor damage from the collapse. But even the WFC buildings without damage effectively became unusable, because for many months, you had to cross through or around the devastation to get there. Like many companies, Amex in New York was immediately homeless. My regular bi-weekly visits to the office stopped because there was no office.

I visited New York again in early November, to check on my place in Jersey City, but I also went into the city. One of the strangest moments of that visit was while walking up a giant plywood ramp the city had constructed on Fulton Street, leading up to a temporary viewing deck in the intersection of Fulton and Church Street, where you could look out at the still-steaming hole where the Trade Center used to be.

St. Paul's Chapel is a beautiful church and an out-of-place anomaly, being standard late-1700s church-sized, now surrounded by giant buildings, like the old man's house in the movie Up. On that day it was gray and rainy, basically the dictionary definition of somber gloom, and walking up that ramp the only thing to look at was the cemetery behind the church, which ran the length of the block parallel to Fulton. Normally green grass under healthy trees, the leaves were now down for winter, and the dust had completely covered the cemetery ground and killed everything. This was close enough to ground zero that materials and objects from the buildings had fallen here, though by that point most of that had been picked up. But as I kept walking up the ramp, I noticed that there were window blinds from one of the buildings stuck in the treetops above the cemetery. If that place had been a sound, it would have been the lowest open note on a cello, bowed with no beginning and no end.

During that trip I also went to the temporary office Amex had set up in New Jersey. My first in-office day after 9/11 was Monday, November 12. At 9:45am, I was talking to my co-workers in their cube farm when people started murmuring about an airplane crash. It was American Airlines Flight 587 that had just gone down in Queens on takeoff from JFK, but at that point we had no idea why. In what remains my most unfiltered use of profanity in any workplace, standing there among the cubicles, I said loudly to what was surely the entire floor, "you have got to be fucking kidding me".

I never ended up meeting the guys to view the documentary, and I've never seen Tom and Jim again. I hadn't thought about it until now, but apparently I'm the sort of person who, if I make a plan that's interrupted by a terrorist attack that kills thousands of people, I'm not in a rush to reschedule. I've never watched the movie again, but I will soon.

With the kind of coincidence that could be used to support the argument that I'm living in a simulation, many years later, in 2013, it was a contact from my work at American Express that brought me into the advertising company where I eventually became CTO. They were a global company with offices in many cities, and multiple offices in New York, but my office was 195 Broadway. The building had been built in 1916 by AT&T to serve as their headquarters, after acquiring the Western Union Telegraph company. It has an important and inspiring place in technology history, as the office of Alexander Graham Bell, and the site of numerous communication firsts, including the first transcontinental and transatlantic telephone calls.

I mention it here, because the side of 195 Broadway runs along most of the block on Fulton, directly across the street from St. Paul's Chapel, where I once walked up that ramp. 15-plus years after 9/11, I regularly walked down that same street, or looked out on that same view from a window above. The blinds in the trees had long been removed, and the cemetery was green and beautiful, and the streets in the neighborhood were packed with people again. The construction on the Trade Center site completed many milestones while I worked there, from the memorial fountains, the stunning Calatrava Oculus train station, the Freedom Tower, and many new office buildings.

A hotel I stayed at a lot for work in the late twenty-teens is on the south side of the trade center site. One morning I was eating breakfast at their top-floor restaurant before work, sitting at a window table on the east side, and I looked down 20 floors below, to the roof of the fire station at 124 Liberty Street. At 7:30am on a random Thursday, the roof was empty except for two things. A giant tractor tire, and a lone man who was flipping it five feet at a time down the length of the roof.

This is the FDNY "Ten House", home of FDNY Engine 10 and Ladder 10. They are the closest fire house to the WTC, directly across the street. Search them and read their stories.

Try to appreciate this image. The scale of the surrounding neighborhood might be the most epic of any city on earth. Almost all of the buildings are between 20 and 100 floors. From above, people on the street are like ants. The fire station is two or three stories, so this guy flipping the tire is surrounded by a massive glass arena of buildings containing people for whom he might die to help, who can look down on him doing his one-task workout as they sip their morning coffee.

The tire-flipper would be a literal Sisyphus, engaged in perpetual and purposeless self-punishment. Except that 9/11 made it clear that his effort is not purposeless. All of the tech and engineering at our disposal, and when bad things happen in that neighborhood, our best option is to send a small team of people like this guy, who have made it their mission to be prepared to climb, carry, and, if necessary, sacrifice.

A few weeks later, after work, I was in O'Hara's, the bar just behind the fire station. I was talking to the bartender and ended up showing him a grainy zoomed picture I'd taken of the tire-flipper on the roof next door, and he said "ha, that's *so-and-so...* he feckin looks just like Bahney Rubble. Built like a feckin fire plug, he's gotta see this, I'll go get him... Flipping a feckin tire, ha ha ha."

We are some durable and hopeful motherfuckers. And I will forever <3 New York.

6

Miscellaneous Technical Topics

The Paradox of Technical Experience

I'm not a bowler, but I've probably bowled maybe two to three hundred times. I know enough to realize that the sweet spot is just to the side of the headpin, and that due to the unique compound-scoring model, closed frames, specifically strikes, are absolutely required for any game that's not languishing at or below 100. I understand enough to know that the difference between nine pins and ten pins is far more than 10%.

Recently one of my brothers has gotten seriously into bowling. He bought a couple of custom balls, one of which was selected to maximize an insane first-ball curve. One night recently I went bowling with him. It was a Saturday night, and we were surrounded by kids' birthday parties, with loud music and a seizure inducing light show. Afterward, I shared my struggles with making modest tweaks to my game, namely hitting more than the far corner 10 pin each roll. And then he launched into one of the more interesting speeches I've heard in the last few years, like a Ted talk delivered by a wildly gesturing intoxicated carny.

The central theme was all about lane oil patterns. A truth of which I had no idea before that moment was that properly maintained bowling lanes are oiled before use, which could be the start of the day for a public bowling alley, or before competition. The pattern starts from a rectangle that runs down the middle of the lane, stopping some variable distance short of the first pin, and which may or may not leave space along the gutters. What follows is a physics Master Class.

On oil, the path of the ball is entirely determined by original launch trajectory, spin, velocity, and weight. When the ball leaves the oil, it picks up significant friction from the wood, and surface properties of the ball, like texture and cleanliness, go from little to high relevance.

In the best case (apologies to bowlers who really understand this, I'm doing my best) the ball uses it's time on the oil to get that full-lane-width wicked curve, and then uses the unoiled bare wood in front of the pins to get "bite" to help bring the force in at an angle. While clearly it's possible to get strikes with a ball rolled straight down the lane, physics and math have determined that coming in at an angle is significantly more effective and error-tolerant, so that's largely what the pros do.

However, if you're playing the curve game, the position of the oil pattern matters tremendously to where you stand to start, how far you launch the ball, your approach to spin, and your target location. And there are people who can work all that out, and do it perfectly or nearly so, again, and again, and again.

But the rest of us dipshits are just rolling balls down approximately the middle of the lane, high fiving for eight pins, burning our mouth on shitty pizza, and hoping the next song that comes on is also ABBA.

In any complex domain, like technology, or… smh… bowling, there are the things you think are the critical problems at the beginning, and then there are the things you start to realize are the true challenges as you begin to really understand the discipline.

I've made this statement probably a thousand times, and I still think it's a great bit of observational advice for anyone in the early stages of the technology systems learning process.

When you first start, 100% of the problem is *getting it to work*.

On your journey to really knowing what you're doing, you ultimately realize that getting it working is the easiest 10% of the problem, and the other 90% is everything else.

- Getting it to work absolutely reliably, so neither you nor anyone else has to keep fucking with it.

- Considering your deployment approach in every decision made about components and technologies to use, so that you waste as close to zero time as possible on operational steps when you need to make changes.

- Architecting for maintainability. Yes, I'm intentionally saying "architecting" because this isn't just about commenting your code. There are innately over-complicated design patterns, like almost anything Object Oriented, that make the process of understanding all of the code that's fired when button X is clicked an entirely unnecessary Odyssey-scale journey.

- Anticipating how the system will age and architecting to minimize pain points. A simple example, if your app includes a high-resolution activity log, and you put that inside your primary app database and build your activity reports there, this will eventually fuck you or whoever you bequeath this to. There are hundreds of potential items like this.

A consequence of this evolution is that you sound increasingly pessimistic. Instead of it'll-be-so-cool-when-it-*can*…, you *seem* to become the *how can this fuck us* guy. I emphasize *seem* here, because that's simply the perception of people that don't know enough to think this way yet. These kinds of questions only sound pessimistic to people who didn't assume they were part of the work to start. To someone like me, delivering all of it, everything the stakeholders asked for **and** everything that being great technology *requires*, is the same project.

Mastery is:

- Selecting tools and ways to work not because they're all you know, but because they'll allow you to deliver the system in the least amount of time, at the highest possible quality.

- Being able to invest the maximum possible portion of your implementation time on *meaningful innovation*, and not repetitive work, operational overhead, troubleshooting meta problems, like environment issues, etc.

- Being able to build things that do not need you to help run them.

To throw down the challenge gauntlet, if you think of yourself as senior, but you tolerate a slow dev environment, or an onerous code-run-test loop, or a too-many-steps house-of-cards deployment process, to name a few of the many components that are as, or more, important than whatever you're being asked to build, then you, my friend, are not.

Integrate with Existing Code Early

The context here is an existing app and codebase, where you're adding a radical change that includes something that's moderate-plus technically complicated.

Examples could be:

- Changing your UI framework.

- Changing your app back-end.

- Changing your data platform.

- Adding real-time something-something, a new data visualization capability, a different client-side state or data layer, etc.

The problem I'm going to describe is less of an issue with non-visual changes, like swapping back-end elements, but even then it's not zero of a problem.

Imagine you have an app where location is relevant, so you decide to explore a sockets-based real time map using GPS to show the user's location, and an icon representing something hurtling toward the user, be it a drone dangling a Carl's Jr order, or a Medicaid-eligible gig-economy ambulance, which is some dude with a CPR certification in a Dodge Caravan with a cot in the back, the Uberlance, if you will.

For a lot of reasons, you will be inclined to build a PoC of the new real-time mapping functionality completely independently from your existing codebase. While I can understand that rationale, the OCG advice is "do not do that".

Here's where it gets tricky. Yes, you should not fuck up your real codebase with every blue-sky fuck-around experiment. That would be silly and wrong, yes, even... no... *especially* when the CTO does it.

However, there's a point where you're fucking around with your new shiny feature that people are going to say "this is amazing... have you shown [insert name of some fuck that matters]", and your display-only no-engine prototype car is suddenly being scheduled for races.

The number of times I've seen this fuck people is in the high millions. I don't have judgement or blame, I understand and applaud the enthusiasm that gets you into these situations. But I'm warning you, down that path there be danger.

Once someone who is not an implementer sees the working shiny, their first thoughts are never, "Stephanie did this over the weekend, so in spite of how functional it seems to be, there's probably a shit ton more work to do to make this really usable."

No. They think "I'm going to sell this motherfucker to our most important customer *today.*"

The problem is that the process of integrating the new advanced shit into your existing codebase may absolutely fuck you.

Assuming you're working with a less aggressive product, sales, or leadership team, there's still a very significant risk that you're the dipshit. I've seen this happen, no details (no, people that know me professionally, this isn't about you), but it's very easy to create a new major feature that works great in a no-context PoC sandbox, but is a buggy unusable dog when you integrate it with the rest of the application. Imagine a scenario where something very cool is built over three, four, five Agile sprints, it looks fully done, people are excited, external demos have happened, and the only thing left is the "integration sprint" where you embed it in the full app and roll it out. And then everything that can go wrong does, like discovering remnants of a femur in the sausage maker after you've just run a large batch.

So, always create your new magic *integrated with the existing codebase* and *never demo to anyone off of localhost.*

There's nothing more fun in software development than having the opportunity to make something really cool that you *know* will blow minds, and even better if you can bang it out in an all-nighter or over the weekend. However, [picture me in a rocking chair on a porch, with a guitar, a basset hound, and a corn-cob pipe that I'm pointing at you with emphatic stabbing gestures] mark my words, *do not delay integration.*

Or say out loud, while working overnight, "I'm excited to see how this fucks me."

People Who Do Not Know Basic Stats About Their Project Irritate Me

This is one of those things that people early in their career would likely not believe happens, but it happens all the fucking time.

Yes, if you work for a big SaaS or a social site, critical performance stats like total subscribers or monthly active users (MAU) will likely be readily available and well known. But for most apps and systems, metrics are either a neglected afterthought, or narrowly focused on a few Truly Impressive Tech Stats used by your leadership team to win hospitality suite "mine's bigger" pissing contests at conferences.

I have been in exactly this conversation a nausea-inducing number of times:

Them: "This data migration is our most critical project. When we finally get fully on the { insert name of a cloud provider or one of the same rotation of data and analytics products }, our joy every day thereafter will put Rome's best orgy to shame."

Me: "Uh, sure. How big is the data."

Them: "What."

Me: "How much data needs to be moved?"

Them: "The fuck would you ask something like that."

Me: "Well, you're saying this is really important, and doing it quickly really matters. One of the single biggest factors affecting how long it takes to move will be how large and complicated the database is. So…"

Them: "You cheeky prick."

Me: "Number of rows… total bytes… how many tables, procs…"

Them: [To the rest of their team] "You also wanna know how much a unicorn's soul weighs? Can you believe this guy."

The *reason* these kinds of properties are good to know is a) to have an order-of-magnitude sense of scale and volume of activity, b) so you have some visibility into the rate of change of those stats so you know if and when you may experience cost, performance, or out-of-resources down-time, and c) so you have a data-driven way to describe what you do in a positive fucking light.

I have had people talk to me about planning for a "big data" platform migration who did not realize their SQL Server database was only 20GB.

Test this yourself and post the results in a comment on any of my videos. Think of the most obvious "probably good to know" stats about whatever you're working on and ask someone you think should know. I'd bet 20% success or less.

To be fair, as stupid as this may sound, knowing these stats is legitimately not straightforward, and unless you do what I'm going to suggest below, even if you do know some of them, it might have been as a one-off at a single point in time, which means today you know fuck all.

So here's a solution. Make a report that gets emailed out every week or month, that lists every significant app, with these key stats. You can eye-roll about email all you want, but this is meant to be super-convenient potty-reading to make sure people get value from it in a quick glance. A high-gloss dashboard where people have to look at a bar, then look at a y axis scale, and do math in their head to know the fucking number, is not prioritizing the proper design principles.

To get you started, here is a list of shit that is probably helpful for you to know about the systems you work on. Obviously, not all of these apply to every system. For example, if the system is an analytics database used by exactly four data scientists, and you send out a report that has "Users: 4" for 37 weeks in a row, you're just giving people new reasons to question your already paper-thin credibility.

For any data platform or app with a database:

- How many rows in the largest table.

- How many total bytes in the largest table.

- How many total rows across all tables.

- How many total bytes across all tables.

- [If reporting] Average number of reports run each day.

- How many tables.

- How many other database objects.

Pro tip: providing a single big number across all of your apps, for any metric, is extremely helpful for managers trying to convince their managers to make a bigger investment in your team.

For apps with users:

- Total number of active user accounts.

- Average daily users (both accounts, and anonymous, if applicable)

- Total number of distinct users active in last week, last month, last 90 days.

- What are the peak and lowest usage times of day, week, month.

- Total active users (or transactions) during peak times.

- Average return visits from the same user by week or month.

- How many support tickets you processed.

For apps with active feature development:

- For every major new feature that rolls out, daily, weekly, monthly access stats. You will be amazed at how much of the shit you build, some of which were "critical features to save this one client", is not being used.

Yes, it would be great to have calculations showing changes for each metric over a relevant time period, but the problem this creates is that since these stats are largely point-in-time, to do day-over-day or week-over-week trends (for example), you would need to store each stat for each time period, because the underlying source data keeps changing (yesterday's number is no longer available today). Setting up a place to store history is *also* a good idea, but don't let having *some* stats end up blocked by designing the perfect metrics capture solution and turning it into a big project that never gets prioritized. People can look at last week's email, and today's email, and do the math in their heads for now.

And for you managers using this book like "ManagementGPT for Lazy Fucks", definitely *do not* just send this list to your team and say, "I want a report with all of these metrics for all of our apps by Monday". "Where did that dipshit get this idea, I never thought they were that smart... this fucking *sucks*" will be what they say about you in the unauthorized unofficial not-work-but-for-work free guerilla Slack instance where all of the real conversations happen. I know Terry said they shut that down, but Terry did not shut that down.

Instead, my suggestion is to ask for three or four of the easy ones. Say to your team, "take a look at this list, and try to pull some of the easy ones and send them to me, but don't turn this into a big project, we have other important shit to do, like build this critical thing product says is the only way to keep Starbexxon-Cola from cancelling our contract, but they really mean it this time."

The Time the Germans Gave a Lightsaber to an Orangutan

A lot of people don't know this story, but in 2007 the Germans successfully prototyped a completely functional lightsaber (or "Lichtschwert"), and then promptly gave it to a non-captive Sumatran orangutan.

If we rewind for a minute to establish historical context, the late 20th century Germans were coming off a hell of a problematic epoch. Rumor has it that the trouble started on New Years Eve in a bar in Paris in 1899, when a group of rowdy Americans were being harangued relentlessly by a cadre of post-enlightenment French proto-communists on the topic of nineteenth century United States fuckery. Precisely who yelled it has been lost to history, but whether it was a French "your" or a Yank "our" is outside of the scope of our story. What *does* matter is that someone in that seedy tavern made the in-spirit statement, interpreted as bombastic challenge, that "*no nation on earth shall ever exceed the level of 1800s American fuckery*". To which, of course, the assembled young Germans, more than one future

Kaiser in their ranks, ominously replied *"halt unser Bier, mein Schnuckiputzi"* ("hold our beer, my sweetiepie").

By the 1990s the Germans were glad to still be at the plate after two undebatable strikes, and more than content with closing out the 1900s in brilliant humility. Their science was highly advanced but understated, the product of over five decades of post-war policy that could best be summarized as "even-if-you-fuck-around-you-won't-find-out" vibes.

During this period, the German national science program tended toward a strange combination of profoundly advanced technological innovation, tempered with Monty Python-caliber absurdity.

"Can't be a weapon if it's funny," they said.

In 2006, they knew they were close when Jurgen Shultz cut off his own left hand while fucking around with what he thought was his cubical-partner's clickable ball-point pen. In fact, it was a synthetic crystal laser hooked up to a 300 gigawatt micro reactor. It had begun working only moments earlier, at which point the primary inventor and work-husband of Herr Shultz, Lars Frankenlieben, had thoroughly shat his own pants and thus decided to take his break early.

If the light saber had been invented by an American corporation, a few key details of our story would be different.

First, within the initial 72 hours, at least one white American man would have cut another man's penis off. Due to a wager, anger, or a dare, with alcohol certainly a considerable factor, this would 100% happen. One hundred percent. The 72 hours is the only part of this that's dubious... and it's a hedge, because I'd bet my kneecaps that it would happen in the first three hours. [To the kid that's shaking my book in the air as an anarchic retro I-told-you-so directed at a post-penis-amputation press conference 39 minutes after your future still-shitty-but-in-a-different-way version of Twitter shared rumblings and rumors about some dingus with a working light saber, I say "mazel tov".]

Second, it would be handled by no less than twenty people, again, still all men, who will make the bzhzhzhzhzhzh sound with their mouths but be way, way too afraid to turn it on.

And finally, under no circumstances would the American corporation have given the first fully operational light saber to a fucking orangutan.

During the investigation afterward, it was discovered that the plan to give the light saber to the orangutan was the product of a resentment-based wager. The invention of the light saber by Dr. Frankenlieben had cloaked the German national science team in an icy pall. Frankenlieben's colleagues were world renowned and eminently accomplished. However, Frankenlieben's invention shattered the long-impenetrable barrier between bleeding edge scientific innovation and concepts that the average schmuck could possibly understand. Frankenlieben's colleagues, who had collectively cured AIDS, seven kinds of cancer, and a podiatric condition known as "gang toe", knew they would never invent anything a tenth as cool as an actual fucking light saber.

Fear, based on the inevitable future where their distinguished careers would be summarized with "oh, you worked at the place where Frankenlieben invented the lightsaber", set in quickly and deeply. Lunch conversations, previously jovial, descended into emphatic "something must be done" table pounding followed by silent brooding bordering on French.

Many were the fingers that pointed, and while accounts varied tremendously, it was Glücklich Kitzler who was fingered most often. Fraulein Kitzler, it seems, was the first to propose the primate trials, which would likely have proven problematic in any scenario, but more condemningly, was also the first, and tellingly the only, scientist to propose that the unfortunately named "Jabroni", known as J.B. for short, should wield the new device.

Jabroni, at six feet of height and two hundred five pounds of mass, the official statement explains, was selected for his close size comparison to a human adult. However, two less desirable charac-

7

Datum, Data, Database

This section will definitely not be everyone's cup of tea. I made a video where I talked about data and queries in simple terms, and I thought it would be a good use of the book medium to elaborate. If a discussion of databases is not something that interests you, feel free to skip ahead to the next section on AI. If you're in sales... just kidding, no one in sales is still reading this book.

Required Historic Context
Before the Database Chapters

If you know about data and database solutions from 1990 until about 2007, feel free to skip ahead. The irony of that statement is that the people least likely to skip ahead are the sumbitches who know and who want to hear a fellow "veteran" tell the war stories. You kids who've only known the anarchy of

NoSQL should take a break and let the silverbacks talk for a minute.

There are a lot of resources out there by people more qualified than I am to tell the story of the early years of personal computers, so I'm going to stick with a few highlights.

The term "personal computer" itself is interesting. The "IBM Personal Computer" was first released in 1981, in a world made up primarily of mainframe and other central-servers with dumb terminals, used for business. And Apple, Tandy, Commodore computers (the "1977 Trinity", look it up) were targeted at a small market of consumers. By 1981, the term "personal computer" meant both "for personal use", and "it works independently from any other computer or network, all the shit you need comes with it". I'm calling this out, because this was the beginning of our modern era, where people started to envision a world where people would each have their own individual computer, for work and for home.

The IBM XT came out in early 1983, and IBM was dominating the growing business market. And then at the SuperBowl in 1984, Apple released a commercial that framed the personal computer battle as "soul-killing homogenized operations" vs "the future of human creativity", which we still see in the positioning of Windows and Mac today. If you haven't seen the commercial, search "1984 Apple's Macintosh Commercial", it still has serious holy-fucking-shit vibes forty years later. I won't insult you with a URL or QR code, we all know how that would go.

In practical reality, in 1990, when I started my first job, at Putnam Berkley, a major NYC-based publishing company, businesses were in a wide variety of states-of-adoption of the personal computer. It shouldn't be a surprise that a big factor was the industry and revenue scale, with technology and money-focused businesses making the investment much earlier than everyone else.

There were still a lot of mainframes and other dumb-terminal solutions like VAX machines, and they were used for most data systems, from air ticketing and baggage, to stock exchanges, to inventory management for companies big enough to have moved off paper, because networking and coordinating multiple individual computers was still extremely primitive or non-existent.

The easiest way to understand these dumb-terminal systems is strangely enough their parallel to the world wide webs. It was the same basic architecture, where you have data and logic stored on a central server, and then light clients that receive data and render it for a user. But these systems were way fucking simpler. The "clients" were screens and keyboards with effectively zero compute capability, and 100% of the processing and logic happened on the central server. User presses a key, it's sent to the server, server figures out if they changed a value or sent a command, does the work, and returns instructions that paint the new screen. The terminals were not computers, all of the users were using a single central computer, and only input and output were handled by the terminals. In 2023, it's hard to find the words to explain this as simply as it was.

The Apple MacIntosh computers were largely not present in businesses at that point, but you were starting to see trickles of adoption in design teams, because of the hugely advanced visual wysiwyg features and the mouse, compared to DOS character-based computers. Windows 1.0 had been out since 1987, but it was shit, in part because it was implemented as an optional interface on top of a fundamentally DOS machine. You would boot to DOS, and then have to run Windows as a separate program from the command line, which would be like asking a designer to crack a bank safe with a stethoscope before every work session.

Personal computer adoption at a business typically started with one or two machines in a shared location, probably a windowless utility room in the center of the building, and people not intimidated by the sorcery would use them for a few hours at a time, and it was those early experimenters that would baby-step trial-and-error their way to understanding how the machine could be used for the business. At my company, I was one of those people, and I spent many hours in 1991 hunkered over an IBM AT.

At my desk, and at everyone else's desks, were IBM Correcting Selectric II typewriters, upon which I wrote probably 500 pages of memos. I still have a soft spot for those machines. The *chunk* sound, which vibrated through your hands when you typed each letter, is the proper level of gravity and authority with which all words and phrases should be composed. Every time you wrote a 50-cent price change memo, it felt like you were creating the Magna Carta. And when you fucked up and backspaced, the *ker-chunk-ker-chunk* alerted everyone in the office. A regular sequence of thought would be:

"Fuck, I misspelled the name at the beginning of the sentence and the correct spelling is a different number of letters, so I can't just fix that word. The only solution is to backspace the whole line or rewrite the whole memo. Fuck. *ker-chunk-ker-chunk ker-chunk-ker-chunk   ker-chunk-ker-chunk   ker-chunk-ker-chunk ker-chunk-ker-chunk   ker-chunk-ker-chunk   ker-chunk-ker-chunk...*"

One other cool detail: that typewriter model, released in 1973, is actually where the concept of our modern backspace key comes from. Before that, the backspace key just moved the type head position back one character, but to remove the prior typed letter, you would need to roll the page up and use white out. On the Selectric II, there was a second tape cartridge for correction tape (the first being the ink). When you hit backspace, it would move the head back, and activate the correction tape. You would then type the previously typed wrong letter, and it would re-strike it, using the correction tape instead of the ink tape. The correction tape was sticky tape designed to work with the carbon powder ink, and it would just lift off the bad character. Take a moment to pick up the nearest computer and give that non-mechanical backspace key a long, sweet kiss. It's the lightsaber to my IBM typewriter backspace's butter knife.

I'm sharing this level of detail to try to put you back into that moment, so you can understand what an order-of-magnitude leap it was at that time to have the opportunity to work on a computer. It's like we were digging a ditch with a spoon, and a dude rolled up with a backhoe.

In one of my favorite movies, *Hidden Figures*, when Octavia Spencer's character, Dorothy Vaughan, who leads the team of human "computers", doing math on paper and sharing it via typewriters, recognizes that the new mainframe is a threat to her and her team's jobs, and seizes the opportunity to sprint at this inevitable future by upskilling and self-study, I see the beginning of my own story. Other than the fact that I was a math-challenged white man working for a New York publishing company in 1991, not a genius black woman in the pre-civil rights era south working for a government agency trying to put a human on the moon. But other than those details, it's like looking into a mirror.

Word processing programs like WordStar and WordPerfect meant that you could change a prior line, paragraph, or page, and everything else just reflowed smoothly. This was all still ASCII-only screens, you only saw plain text, and you added codes to tell it to print with bold, underline, or italics. The alternative, however, as previously mentioned, was a fucking *typewriter*.

But the GOAT, the difference maker, the heart breaker, the undertaker, was Lotus 1-2-3, the best early spreadsheet for the IBM computers. This was still running on ASCII MS-DOS, so it was visually simple as fuck, but let me tell you, using a spreadsheet for the first time when all you've really known is ink on paper was like being the one monkey that knows how to fly the banana drone.

A lot of you motherfuckers are walking around picturing data in rows and columns like that's an innate and timeless property of the universe, but someone had to invent that shit. And another dude had to think to themselves "rows and columns are great, but what if we could do *math* with that shit". "I'd like to do the same shit to every value in just this one column" was again, another example of something that is not inherent or in any way natural, but some fucking hero made that work. [These aforementioned dudes and heroes were Dan Bricklin and Bob Frankston, the creators of Lotus 1 2 3 precursor, VisiCalc.]

Lotus 1-2-3 was the PC's killer app, and there were articles in the mid-80s saying that IBMs advantage wasn't DOS compatibility, but "1-2-3 compatibility". Innovations in expanding RAM capacity were primarily driven by the need to support customers working with large 1-2-3 spreadsheets. A hypothetical /r/rowscols reddit from the late 80s would have read like a *Wolf of Wall Street* live blog, but with way more math, STDs, and cocaine.

I appreciate that you people can load up Unreal and build an entire world between school and dinner, but please, please, have respect for those upon whose shoulders you stand.

Lotus 1-2-3 had one other feature that I discovered, and it was ultimately my *pulling Excaliber from the rock under a beam of light from the sky* moment. Those same Lotus hero geniuses also thought to themselves, "I bet a lot of people end up doing sequences of the exact same steps, like formatting specific cells, adding formulas to every row, etc., so what if we make our command structure very clear from our menu, and give them a really easy way to play back sequences of commands…"

Yes, the first "programming" I ever did was with Lotus 1-2-3 macros. In hindsight, this is both funny, and thematically significant in my tech career. From day one, I've only ever learned anything for the purpose of solving a specific problem I was having right fucking now. To this day I've never taken a class or a course. Other than accidentally, I've never learned any aspect of technology in the abstract, and then later went out searching for a problem to solve with my new knowledge. In every case, I've stood at a fork in the road where I could use what I already know, which, in front of that IBM AT in that hot back room in 1991, it was how to manually edit and format cells in a spreadsheet, or, I could see a glimpse of a way to do it more easily by automating the repetitive steps. "I could either do this manually in two hours, or take thirty hours to figure out how to automate it, with a significant risk that my whole approach is flawed to the point of total impossibility. I might also need to buy something expensive that may not work, and that I cannot use for any other purpose." If you're reading this, you already know both the right answer, and my answer.

If this were a Kung Fu movie, and I'm hoping it is one day, this would be the montage scene where you see me sitting alone with primitive computers and increasingly thick books. The audio would be just the instrumental of "I'm Broken" by Pantera, overlayed with me just saying "fuck" ten thousand different ways. The only physical activity would be page turning, typing, and crying.

Spreadsheets unlocked a federated data revolution, but they were still ultimately document-based, which meant whole document reads and whole document writes. Only one person could edit them at a time, which limited them to single-user use cases, or people yelling "who has the file open... dammit Roger, I asked you and you said no, but I can fucking see it right there on your screen... I need to do my updates before Tammy gets back from lunch... ok five more minutes, but I'm serious, I'll unplug you again."

The answer to this problem came in the form of file-based databases, like dBase and derivatives. This is foreshadowing a later discussion about query optimization, but the magic in dBase was using fixed column and row sizes, which enabled in-place multi-user updates. Given that each non-character data type (int, numeric, date) is stored in a specific number of bytes, if you also require character columns to be a fixed length, then the schema of the table tells you the byte coordinates for any single row-column value in the table. For example, if the "name" column is 30 bytes wide and starts at byte 20 in each row, and the total bytes reserved for every row is 500, then dBase could calculate the exact position on disk for every name value, for every row. To update the name for the third row, you could just directly overwrite the 30 bytes at position 1020.

This predictable structure allowed for concurrency, because the data was no longer treated like a document and loaded or saved as a single unit. Remember that this was still a file-based data store, so each "table" was a file with a dbf extension, sitting on a local disk or on a network share.

This brings us to the late 1990s. The ability to for a moderately skilled person to make a dBase, FoxPro, FileMaker, or Microsoft Access database, and create a much more sophisticated system than simple spreadsheets, had resulted in incredible proliferation of do-it-yourself solutions and figure-it-out amateur technologists. The figure-it-out people were typically connected to a business unit, and not a formal tech org, and there started to be a bifurcation in non-tech companies where tech orgs did infrastructure, like networking, file shares, and PC management, and the guerilla rebels began working on increasingly sophisticated databases and applications. This was typically not a copacetic relationship, because being involved in the high-value, high-visibility, differentiating systems made you more valuable, and made it easier to get resources. Formal tech orgs started to feel, and actually become, marginalized as more and more high-value, high-visibility systems were developed and managed directly by the business teams.

In my opinion, the battle between these empowered business-first teams, and traditional technology-first teams, is the healthiest, greatest, worst, most fucking frustrating relationship in our discipline, and I love it. And hate it. Mostly love. But ask me again in a few minutes.

I personally worked on an analytics system in 1998 for American Express, with tens of millions of rows in a multi-file FoxPro solution. When we ran monthly reporting, there was a small army of PCs deployed with papers taped to the screens, ready to be flipped down as a warning "Do Not Disturb, Processing...", running for full days at a time. For its time, as nuts as this may sound in hindsight, from a cost, ease-of-management, and value to the business perspective, it was a really great system.

However, there was a point where the data size and processing load across multiple file-based systems began to hit limitations. One simple one, which is kind of interesting in the context of some of my points in later chapters, was the problem created by the fact that the data was *stored* on static network file shares (a Novell server, I believe), while all of the *processing* was done by network connected PCs. In the client-server database world we're all very familiar with now, the network traffic is limited to a small number of bytes forming the instructions from the client, and the precise requested result set returned from the server.

In a file-share-based model, the server is just dumb storage. When the dBase, FoxPro, and Access clients were querying a table, if a query could be optimized with an index search so that just the bytes from the server-side files for the rows that met the criteria were returned, that worked pretty well. However, if a table scan was needed (a query that could not use an index), the entire table needed to be transported over the network to the requesting client, to be run through row by row.

Eventually, we hit a point of diminishing returns, where the network traffic impact of adding another processing computer would slow down every other processing computer.

It was in this environment I first experienced basic data management and processing principles that I still use regularly today.

Query Optimization

I love database technology so much. Beyond its role in trying to create order and structure, and therefore usability, on content representing our very messy and chaotic world, it's an area where you are easily able to test a brute-force solution side-by-side with something smart and beautiful. For most other areas of general software development, the contrast isn't so simple and clear. Yes, the difference between a shitty web site initialization and a tight one is clear and very satisfying, and there are plenty of app-language optimizations that are night-and-day. But data is the space where most of us experience the majority of our holy shit moments, of turning something unusably awful to something smoking fucking fast, with the smallest of changes.

Most people today cut their data teeth on small datasets running on comparatively hyper-powerful computers. I could port the original dBase file system I described above to SQLite on my phone, and it would probably run faster.

Both the file-based solution, and the Sybase and SQL Server solutions that followed, trained me like a Pavlovian dog being rewarded with Vienna sausages or punished with a shock collar. Tiny adjustments would make the difference of something running for ten hours, or in a few minutes or seconds. Because the dBase processing would effectively lock up your whole computer, there was no "kick it off in the background and run it all day while I work on something else". Taking twenty extra minutes to experiment with optimizations might mean the difference between getting four custom reports out on a given day, or not even finishing one. And there's no way I could accept sitting in front of a frozen computer for more than a few minutes at a time. At least one other person in that room would spent a couple of hours each day waiting on code to run while reading an honest-to-god newspaper.

In the year-and-a-half I was doing that work, I must have done the write-run-cancel-fix loop ten thousand times. When you got it right, the machine would lock while single-tasking, and then return the interactive console in a few seconds. When you got it wrong, you knew after it was hung for two or three minutes, and you cancelled out and tried again.

The critical learning of this period was that query processing time is all about *how much shit you ask it to touch*. That might be direct, like SELECTing with no filter or a filter that just returned a lot of data (country = "US" in a North American CRM). More likely, though, it was indirect, where what you're asking for *should* be a reasonably small amount of data, but either how you asked, or how the data is structured, requires that the query reads through a lot of irrelevant shit to find what you're looking for.

Concept 1: physical stored order matters a whole fucking lot.

This is going to be the bar-stool summary, not the computer science summary. Presumably if you're still reading this, either you don't have access to the internet, or the computer science version made as much practical sense as trying to learn hip-hop dance from an audiobook. You came to the right place. [Gestures to bartender to bring a couple of pickled eggs and two shots of Old Crow... turns stool to face you, and starts talking while making large hand gestures.]

Imagine you have a plain text file open in a text editor with no "Find" feature, with exactly one integer on each line, from one to one million, and you're certain those integers are all in numeric order.

If I asked you to find the number one million, what would you do? Of course, you would just move the scrollbar to the very bottom of the file. Bang, one step, there it is, done!

Next, we try to locate 500,000, and again, like the LeBron of text file navigation, in one step, you move the scrollbar to about the middle, and... holy shit, there it is, right where we expected!

OK, now we take the same file and randomly sort all of the values. First value is 700,341, second value is 9. The whole thing is totally fucked up.

And now I ask you to find the number 500,000...

OK, for fuck sake stop scrolling around. I'm not waiting here while you actually try to find the fucking number. We're simply trying to learn here, and my question is, *what would your repeatable process be to find the number?* With the sorted list, you knew that the largest number would always be at the bottom, and the middle number would be in the middle, so you could just jump right to them. With an unsorted file? Exactly... the repeatable process is to *read through the whole file until you find it.* If it's the third row, then you only had to do three reads, lucky fucking day. But if the number you're looking for is row 980,005... well, I'll check in tomorrow.

Every other thing you need to know about query optimization is a direct extrapolation of what we just learned above. You can test any query strategy against the basic question of "based on how I'm asking, and how the data is structured, how many reads and how much jumping around will need to be done to find and assemble the shit I'm looking for?" At root, it's no more complicated than that.

Other related shit that's useful to understand.

Modern database and analytics software is layer upon layer of brilliant optimizations for ever-more-focused data type, storage, and access scenarios. We're all driving Ferraris, Lamborghinis, and Bugattis now. If you get to the point where you need to set a land-speed record, then you probably want to understand shit like your specific tire performance on surface X at temperature Y. But if you're building a web app to let your coworkers anonymously vote on pet pictures, you can probably hold off on that.

I find it helpful to focus on the things which are generally true, rather than get caught up in a lot of platform-specific details. Once you understand the basics, they should be something you always do, like covering your genitals when you leave your home. That's my bar on this. If I say "indexes" and someone says "premature optimization", it's absolutely no different than if they were to stand during a meeting and reveal their man, woman, or other junk hanging out. Go home and come back when you're ready to build non-shitty software in pants, a skirt, or a fucking toga, our expectations are not insurmountably high.

The concept of an **index** can take a lot of forms, but they all simply act as a sorted entry point for your data. I'll keep using the word "index", though in each data platform the word may vary. For example, "partitions", and "sort keys" represent similar concepts in different platform contexts. Don't let anyone who knows more than you *yeah-but* you down some rabbit hole on this. Yes, there are differences in how these concepts are implemented in different technologies, but for 98% of your likely needs, simply understanding what I'm describing here will really help.

Our sorted million-integer file is a good example of an index. Indexes are always sorted by their values, which is the trait that makes them so useful. This is what enables highly efficient search strategies, like a binary search, versus an inefficient linear search, where you read every value sequentially until you find what you're looking for. Binary search is simply continually jumping halfway in the sorted list, and asking "is the value I'm on larger, smaller, or equal to what I'm looking for". If the value is larger, then the next hop will be to the middle of the top side of the index, if larger, the bottom side, and that same test repeats until you find exactly what you're looking for. Because of the way math works, this halving strategy can find any value in a very large list with relatively few reads. Each platform has a lot of additional optimizations, based on the data type of the index values and statistics that can be stored about value distribution, etc., but the core of it is using the properties of an ordered list to avoid checking every fucking value.

One important index concept which is, of course, confusingly named differently across platforms, is whether the index is the sort order for the actual fucking table (or file), or if it is a list of sorted keys and their associated row positions, stored separately from the table, which does not affect the stored-order of the table itself. To make this easier to understand, I'll use SQL Server as the example.

In SQL Server, a "clustered index" is like any other index, but the way it's stored is by sorting the actual table contents. Imagine a table with a phone number column. If we create a clustered index on phone number, the table will be re-sorted so all values for all rows are in the order of their phone number value.

If that same phone number index was created as a non-clustered index (I'll just call them "indexes" from here out), the phone numbers will be pulled from the table, along with the byte position of the start of the source row in storage (the row corresponding to the specific phone number), and a separate data structure will be generated and stored, ordered by the phone number.

Suppose you run a query "SELECT * FROM person WHERE phone_number = '202-456-1111';".

Using the standard index, the query processor would do a quick search to locate the ordered phone number, and then use that index entry to get the byte position of the row on disk. The processor would then need to do a second read from the row's location on disk to go pull the whole row to return the result.

If phone number was a clustered index, the processor can do the phone number search and the full-row read in the same step, because the phone number search is happening directly on the stored table rows, and when the value is found, the processor is already reading the actual row. The index and the table are essentially the same physical thing, but the only columns in the table affecting the order are the ones specified when creating the index.

One or both of these two variations exist in some form across most data platforms, and it can be helpful to understand how the platform you're using handles this. I think it's also extremely conceptually helpful to appreciate that even though an index may be stored separately from the main content, the overhead of doing a lookup in one place, and then using the very specific location pointers returned by that search to pull individual rows from the main table, is way fucking better than just reading brute force through the main table until you find what you're looking for. A data index is the same concept used in a book index. Yes, it's a slight pain in the ass to flip to the back, lookup a term from an alpha-sorted list, and then flip back to the page number, but the alternative is to read the whole fucking book until you find what you need, and I don't wish that on anyone.

While there can be advantages to having a table physically sorted by a clustered index on systems that support them, the important takeaway here is just to understand that indexes can just be the way the main data is sorted, or they can be a separate thing, and they both work well, but have some use-case-specific nuances.

One of the problems with clustered indexes, which is why products like PostgreSQL don't support them (the one-time CLUSTER command is not the same, *Todd*), is that in order to deal with the fact that an insert could happen at any time into any part of the table, there's a lot of extra apparatus required to ensure that every insert doesn't trigger a full table rewrite. Hopefully this makes sense: if your table is physically sorted by phone number, and you insert 555-555-5555, you'd effectively have to rewrite the bottom half of the table to insert that row in the right place. SQL Server solves this by reserving space throughout the blocks of storage for future inserts.

This "if it's physically sorted then there's some additional shit to consider" truth carries over to other cases. For example, on AWS S3, when storing separate files meant to be queried from Athena, the partitions required to optimize queries are based on the S3 folder/key naming hierarchy. If you have, say, a trillion stored json files each representing an event in an activity log, and you realize you need to change your partitioning approach, you need to rewrite all trillion of the keys/folders, and possibly the files, to make that change.

However, for most relational database cases, just create a PRIMARY KEY constraint on the primary key column, and use CREATE INDEX for other frequently-filtered columns, and you'll be money.

Cardinality, or the number of unique values, is a big consideration in creating and using indexes. The highest cardinality would be a unique primary key, where the value is different for every row. The lowest would be a boolean, where there can only be two different values. With one possible exception that I'll talk about below, creating indexes on low cardinality columns is a bad idea. The query optimizer will almost never use them, and you've added extra write and storage overhead for keeping the indexes up to date.

Creating indexes on unique keys is a no-brainer, and are absolutely necessary in transactional systems where you're frequently retrieving or updating single rows. If CRUD operations are slow, the first thing you should check is to ensure the existence of indexes on the keys. This is also true for columns that aren't keys, but likely contain high-cardinality values, like drivers license number, phone number, etc. but only if they are *frequently the primary filter* in a query. *You should not create indexes on columns that are rarely used in queries.*

Where it gets more complicated are medium-cardinality columns that may be used regularly in queries. Examples of medium cardinality would be U.S. state (~50 options, depending how territories are handled), or a status code with 15 possible values. My advice here is not to create indexes initially on these columns, and wait until you have specific query cases, and then do some trial and error to see what works best. Likely, indexing these columns is closely related to the next concept.

To understand ***index coverage***, let's look at an example. Imagine we have a table named "students", which includes among other things our phone number column, which is used in a standard index, which as we described above, is stored as a separate structure from the main table.

If we run "SELECT phone number FROM students WHERE phone_number='901-332-3322';", this query will be fully "covered" by the index. This means that the processor will scan the index for the phone number value, and then say:

"OK, found it, now what does this fuck want me to do... ok I see, they just want me to return the value of the phone number. That's kind of fucking stupid, but leaving that aside, since the phone_number column is part of the index, then I've already got the value from the index search, so I don't need to access the main table at all. Here you go."

This if-it's-all-in-the-index-I-don't-access-the-table coverage behavior opens up a really nice and easy optimization strategy. Let's imagine a slightly more complex scenario.

Tables "students", "courses", and a many to many table "students_x_courses". Assuming we're not dipshits and we used guids and reasonable names for the PKs, we have "guid_student", "guid_course" and the _x_ table contains both.

Assuming our app will need to show "all of the courses for this student", we get:

SELECT c.guid_course, c.course_name
FROM courses c INNER JOIN students_x_courses sxc
ON c.guid_course = sxc.guid_course
AND sxc.guid_student = 'abc123';

If our students_x_courses table is indexed on (guid_student, guid_course), then this index will *cover* everything we need from the students_x_courses table. This means that the index will be used both to quickly find student 'abc123', AND it will be used to *return the value for the corresponding course guids*. This query will never need to access the actual students_x_courses table.

Had we defined the index as only (guid_student), then it would have been used to find the student rows, but the processer would have also needed to read the corresponding rows from the underlying table to get to the course guids.

The simple rule is that if all of the columns required for an entire query are present in the index, then the processor can service those requirements fully from the index. For this particular use case, which is a many to many mapping table that is primarily queried to find the relationships between the two entity types, by creating a multi-column compound index, you will likely save a good amount of additional read overhead.

In case this isn't clear, indexes take up additional space, and every column you add duplicates that data from the underlying table. There is also overhead in keeping the indexes up to date as values in the table change, and that's made worse the more columns you include in an index.

The ***order of the columns*** in a compound index matters! This is easy to visualize if you think of a spreadsheet containing columns for "state" and "last name". If you sort the spreadsheet by state, then by last name as a second level, and then scroll down trying to find "Johnson", you'll quickly realize that this is fucking impossible. Because state is first, you would need to go to each state one by one, and then go alphabetically "John..." etc 50 fucking times! And Guam and Puerto Rico!

While last name is indexed, because it's the second column in a compound index, it's *totally useless **unless** you're also filtering on state*. In our spreadsheet, if the query was state = "da" (per Randy, store last two char of state for advanced security) and last_name = "Johnson", the sort would work great.

This should definitely be reflected in your indexing strategy. If we consider our students and courses example, remember that our only index is (guid_student, guid_course). This is great for the case where we used it above, to filter on student, to locate the course guids. However, an equally likely use case would be to go the opposite direction, to find all of the students in a single course. For that second query type, our index will be ignored. The solution is to create a second index with the same columns reversed, like (guid_course, guid_student). Now both query types can take advantage of indexed search.

And finally, I'll go one step further, applying everything we've covered so far. It's highly likely in most transactional systems that there is at least one other column that's used in just about every query. Maybe it's a status column, an owner identifier, or a soft delete flag or timestamp. In this case, we're not talking about *every* column that might sometimes be used in a query, we're specifically looking for those one or two extra columns that are *almost always used*. In my case, in transactional systems, I include a delete_when datetime which is used as a soft delete indicator. I use a timestamp instead of a boolean so you know *when* it was deleted, as well as if it is deleted. I default it to 1/1/2050, my standard far-future date, and disallow nulls. So almost every query of every table includes AND delete_when > now(). If you have a column or columns like this, used in all or nearly all queries, be sure to include them in your index.

One other important tip: on most platforms, if a column you're filtering on is part of an expression, if there's an index on the column, it will not be used for the query. For example, LEFT(phone_number,3) = '212' will ignore an index on phone_number, while phone_number LIKE '212%' will usually use the index. Check the docs for your platform to confirm.

So this isn't misconstrued, to really do query optimization well, it **is** important to understand the nuances of the underlying platform. That said, I've found that with MS SQL Server, PostgreSQL, and MySQL, you can largely just follow these recommendations and let the platform own the rest, and it will work pretty well.

Another platform I've used extensively is AWS Redshift, which is PostgreSQL compatible, but is a *columnar* database, and as such is fundamentally different in terms of query methodology than a typical transactional RDBMS. In a columnar database, values are stored by *column* vs by row like a traditional database. This can be a bit hard to wrap one's head around. One way to think about it is that a columnar database essentially creates an index on each column, and that is also the primary storage for that column. On disk, the value for state from the second "row" is stored between the value of state from the first "row" and the value of state from the third "row". If there is another column named last_name, it stored in a separate structure which only contains all of the last name values.

Because each column essentially behaves like an index, and they can be read very quickly as isolated structures, this database type works really well for aggregate queries on very large amounts of data. For example, SELECT count(*) FROM event_log WHERE user_agent = "Windows" will be smoking fast on 20 billion rows. However, SELECT * (or 20, 30, 40 specific columns) is less efficient, because it has to do additional work to correlate the column values to assemble and return them together as rows. You would never use a columnar database for a one-row-at-a-time transactional system.

Tools to Help You Not Biff It

Query plans are your friend. Most database systems have the ability to show you the execution plan for a particular query, which is invaluable when you're trying to figure out why a specific query is slow. Searching "interpreting a query plan", optionally adding the name of your specific platform, will yield a lot of great information, and I won't duplicate that here.

However, it's worth saying the key items in plain English. You can simplify this to two basic scenarios: querying a single table and querying multiple tables using joins or subqueries.

For the comments below, I'm going to use the words "table scan" for the scenario where the query processor just reads through all of the rows in the base table, ignoring any available index. When we read through every row of the unsorted integer file above, we were doing a "table scan". This is the brute-force method to look for shit, and it is always the fallback if no other optimizations are available. It's worth noting that the cost of a table scan can vary, potentially significantly, between platforms. If the platforms shard your data, a table scan may still be parallelizable, where the brute force search can be split up and run on separate compute, each scanning a different section of your table. Don't assume a table scan is *always* bad, but in most cases in large tables on traditional database platforms, it's the red flag that may indicate a problem.

A huge, hopefully obvious tip: while you're working through performance issues, *break a complex query up into parts* and resolve problems in each part before combining them. You could end up going down some subquery rabbit hole, only to later realize that the problem is that your parent-table query isn't using an index. If you have a multi-table query, if it's feasible, try to simplify the problem into the single-table case, get that fast, then move on.

In a single table query, there should really not be more than three factors:

- *Is the table big enough for the processor to get value from the indexes?* This may not be obvious, but if the table is "small" (relative to the platform, so this is variable), the query processor might just say "fuck it, let's scan", because reading 10 rows directly is faster than using an index, then still having to go back to the 10-row table to pull the output.

- *Is there an index that should have relevance for the query?* The *have relevance* point has a bit of nuance. Most of your filter criteria may be represented in an existing index, but if there are problems, like it's a compound index and you're not filtering on the first column in the index, or the index your using has very low cardinality, etc., then it will be ignored.

- *What portion of the total source rows will be in the output?* Again, this may be obvious, but if your query is going to return a third or more of the total rows from the table (the portion is variable based on the overall table size, platform, etc.), and there is no index that can "cover" the selected output columns, the query processor will likely say "fuck it, scan" because the slight filtering advantage of the index won't make up for the overhead of using the index with a lot of valid hits, and then looking those rows up again in the base table.

If you work through the questions above, and your answers are optimization-favorable, you should be able to find a good filter and index combination that makes your query fast.

For multi-table queries, whether via join, subqueries, exists, etc, the optimization process gets a bit more complex.

Assuming your query is running on a lot of data, in the best case, you want to see a plan where the first step dramatically limits the target rows, likely by using an index. This is usually 90% of the hurdle to getting a fast query, because if in step 1, it either needs to read a lot of rows, or worse, it produces a lot of rows to feed into the next step, nothing else really matters, it's going to be slow as fuck.

One concept to make sure we understand is that while yes, the more compound steps involving multiple tables a query has, the more work it *may potentially* have to do, the important factor is **not** *how many* joins or subqueries there are, but what the fuck each of them *are actually doing*.

Taking an example, suppose we have eight tables in a transactional system, representing a central "user" table, and then seven tables ranging from login history, to shit the user has access to, etc. For this example, let's say that for a specific user we want to query, there are between zero and no more than 10 rows in those secondary tables. This is running on a medium instance PostgreSQL server, and each of these tables has fifty million rows.

A query filtering by the user ID on the primary table, which is indexed, and joining to the seven other tables on an indexed foreign user ID key, is going to be fast as fuck. Like run-done fast.

Why it's fast is because of all of the principles we've covered above. This is what these platforms are built to do, and they're fucking great at it. It's a simple a + b = c: if it can use an optimized search method, and there's not much data involved, it should be damn near instantaneous.

Where your slow multi-table query has gone wrong has something to do with one of those basic factors. Either there is no optimized way to find the primary or sub-rows involved, at some level a large number of rows are being touched, or both.

And additionally consider:

- The order of the tables in your FROM clause can matter. Some optimizers take a hint from your query and start from the likely-dubious assumption that you might know what the fuck you're doing. Given that, in a JOIN query, starting with the table that is most filtered to quickly reduce the rows is an obvious fast-path, the optimizer often assumes that you're not too stupid to realize that, so it trusts that the first table in your FROM clause is the most-filtered entry point for the query. However, if you have no fucking idea what you're doing and the order of your FROM clause reflects that, this could be slowing things down. If you have a slow query, experiment with the order of the tables.

- The difference between the performance on production data and a smaller dev database can be a huge part of your SQL performance troubleshooting.

The situation where a query runs quickly on a smaller-volume, lower-activity dev environment, is very common, and troubleshooting this can be difficult due to access constraints for production. Here are a few things that may help:

- Just because the query is fast on dev doesn't mean it's being optimized correctly. It is likely because the amount of data is so small that brute-force reads can go through the entire table very quickly. This is good news, because it means you can start by just applying all of the recommendations above to dev, while monitoring the query plan so you know when the execution switches from brute force table scans to more optimized. When you push that code to prod, with any accompanying index changes, it should be much faster.

- SQL trace logging can be helpful in that your operations team can turn it on, capture a period of performance data, and then share the log with you, to give you some insight to what's happening in prod without giving you access. However, I really don't like this approach, because the learn-change-test process is slow, as presumably you're not running your in-progress queries directly on the prod data environment. If this is your only choice, I'd recommend throwing a tantrum until the admins agree to support the next option.

- Get temporary read-only access to prod and tweak your problem-query directly on the data that's giving it problems. This can be monitored, and your access should be turned off as soon as possible. Highly efficient, and you'll learn a lot.

NOT IN

I made an off-hand joke about this in one of the videos, and it's worth clarifying.

I can't imagine it would ever be reasonable to say that a specific feature in any language should never be used, and this is true about the NOT IN operator. However, NOT IN has the dual properties of being quite useful and intuitive to use, while also being inherently poor performing in many cases.

Expanding slightly, NOT IN usually precedes a subquery, so a more complete example would be something like:

FROM main_table WHERE customer_id NOT IN (SELECT customer_id FROM exclusion_table)

This may look a bit like a JOIN, where you could imagine that we're correlating all the customer_ids from main_table with a single query pulling customer_ids from exclusion_table. But because we're specifying "NOT", we're not finding the matches. Instead we're checking *every customer_id from main_table*, against *every customer_id from exclusion_table* to ensure there are NO matches. As this is structured (by using NOT IN), there's no good way to shortcut this process. Each item in A will be checked against each item in B. The number of tests will then be the count of A times the count of B, which, with even moderate sized tables, gets really big really quickly.

The opportunities where NOT IN might be the best option could include cases where either or both tables have very few rows. In every other case, you should do your best to avoid NOT IN.

Also, because the size of the tables really matters to the query performance, a query that might work well when the system is new may slowly degrade as the table sizes grow. One example would be a query that uses NOT IN (SELECT email FROM users) to prevent adding a duplicate user, which will work great when you have only a few users and be absolute shit when you hit 50,000,000.

The best alternative to NOT IN depends on your data platform, your data volume, the nature of the complete query, and your use case. For example, if NOT IN makes a batch process script a little slower but a lot easier to understand, that might still be the best option. Other alternatives to NOT IN could include:

- NOT EXISTS is usually better optimized but read your database docs to be sure.

- LEFT OUTER JOIN to the exclusion table on the column you're using as the exclusion lookup, with a WHERE exclusion-column IS NULL in the main query. The LEFT OUTER JOIN will return all the rows (excluded or not), and then the WHERE will filter to keep just the non-matches (no corresponding row in the exclusion table). Do a small test on your database platform to ensure you get the expected results.

- Same as the prior LEFT OUTER JOIN approach, but without the WHERE clause, instead parking that first result in a temp table, and then issuing a DELETE statement to remove all of the rows where exclusion-column IS NULL (your final result is the contents of the temp table after the DELETE). This shouldn't perform better, but sometimes does.

Keep in mind, if you just have a lot of shit in table A, and a lot of shit in table B, and you want all of the A rows that aren't in B, that might just be a slow fucking query. Your best option might be to consider storing the information in a different structure, if this is a common query for your app. This is particularly true if only a small number of rows from A ever meet the criteria, and the query supports a UI and needs to be milliseconds.

And finally, anyone who believes COUNT(*) is less efficient than COUNT(1) or any other option, is wrong. Anyone who believes this and says it out loud to correct other people is an ass. If you are one such ass, I recommend fighting the Kraken and your inner demons on one of the multiple highly visited StackOverflow posts dedicated to this topic, and in any event, allow me to RSVP to that discussion as "not interested, but please put me down for five vegan entrees".

8

AI, AI… Oh.

I made a video where I talked about my opinion on the impact of capabilities like ChatGPT and their future iterations on tech careers. But AI is a topic that deserves much broader attention.

I'm probably not the only one that's looked at all the hubbub and dialog around ChatGPT and AI and thought "where I work, we still can't do timesheets right", and then I shake my head skeptically at humanity's prospects while taking the first sip of my third dirty breakfast martini.

The current Large Language Model AIs are largely misunderstood outside of a true tech audience, and as a result, the "LinkedIn Lens" on this can be pretty off the mark. And to be fair, these machines can really seem like they're *thinking*, so it's understandable that CFO Kip Jenbrendensen might draw the conclusion he's talking with Hal or Jarvis.

I'm not going to spend much time rehashing the what-is and how of the current era of services, there is a ton of that out there by people much better qualified than me. However, I have a couple of ways I've been thinking about it that I'll share because it may be useful.

As I type this it's 4:01am Eastern time. I woke up at 2am and ideas immediately started spinning through my head, and finally at 3am I said fuck it and started typing into my phone in the dark.

Given any gap in my focus on a single activity, my brain will start doing this. There was a point earlier tonight, where I was just out of the shower, naked in my bathroom, simultaneously gargling mouthwash and applying preparation H, where my brain bumped up to what must have been meta layer three or four and thought the following.

I'm simultaneously writing literal sentences in my mind for the book, based on a story from New York, because I had been thinking about a different memory from NY, while performing routine maintenance on both my energy input and my waste output ports. And until that instant, though the actions were well underway, I hadn't for a second consciously considered what my hands were doing.

ChatGPT doesn't do that. What I mean by "that" is the constant internal input processing and reflection loop that most of us humans have (no, my point had nothing to do with buttholes, *Kyle*). Most significantly, like the old school interface event loop, our internal loop fires even with no input. While true read stdin and do... *something*.

Knowing that at least 25% of you are on an argument hair trigger on the AI topic, picture me extending both hands toward you, palms open in the universal "easy there... easy buddy..." pose, like you're a velociraptor or a Texan who was forced to go to San Francisco for work. "OCG friend..." points to my own chest, points to your chest.

No, I'm not saying there isn't constant processing in GPT. But there's a distinction between processing done for an individual chat endpoint instance and processing *at any more general level*. When you ask GPT a question, after it answers you, it immediately stops giving a shit about you. It's not going to text you two hours later and say, "on second thought maybe we *did* land on the moon... and do you have any more of that weed". Don't get me wrong, a programmer could, and most certainly *will*, for the same reason some fuckwit programmed the robocaller, keep the virtual sessions alive. They could launch timers to periodically do pre-determined stuff like run your prompts again, and then run a "summarize the differences" prompt between your earlier results and now, and then send you a "u up had more thoughts..." dm on every platform you're connected to, thus becoming your super smart but socially fucked up machine friend who you chat with a lot but would never, ever invite to stuff.

A good analogy is the guy from Memento with anterograde amnesia, storing and restoring state every few minutes using his tattoos. Neither are the *same* as a continuous self-aware consciousness, and this creates some substantial limitations for A-"I".

AGI, artificial *general* intelligence, isn't necessarily what I'm talking about either. You could have a general intelligence that can "remember" you between sessions, continue a conversation, and even ask you six months later if you regret breaking up with Roger after that unfortunate tequila fueled LOTR and Star Wars argument last Cinco de Mayo. But if that bot state is reloaded from storage every time you want to talk, vs staying fully online and venting to other bots between sessions about your obvious narcissism and chronic pattern of bad decisions, no matter how many digits of pi or New Yorker-caliber articles it can spew, It. Is. Not. Thinking.

The reason this matters is... myriads of reasons. But mainly, once a company (it won't be "a group of randoms" or a university...

this is space-program expensive) creates an AGI, there will be an arms race and humanity will almost certainly lose. But hold that thought.

Let's talk about *now*. We've got some decent image and video AI which effectively amounts to nothing more than fast automated photoshop and CGI. Deepfakes have been possible for a while if you wanted to invest the time. From what I've seen of the "art", it's fast but not novel.

True side-story tangent. I once had a startup that was growing so fast, we kept adding office space, generating a lot of depressing bare walls. I approached a local college art professor and painter who had a ton of 30-year-old abstract paintings piled in his storage unit. I made what I thought was a creative and fair offer, to buy two paintings at his asking price, but to get eight additional paintings on loan to hang in the office for one year, with great exposure and the potential for more sales. Thinking I'd buy the two anyway, he declined.

Instead, I went to an art supply store, and for far less money, bought a dozen large canvases and quarts of non-toxic elementary school paint, and had my 18-month-old son channel his inner Pollock and bang out some art. The result were paintings that brought life and joy to those office walls, and my home, for more than 15 years now. In most OCG videos, you can see a photo on the wall behind me of my son, in a diaper, doing that painting, during one of our forced toddler labor sessions. Fuck that professor, I hired a baby.

The ability to copy, literally or in spirit, from prior human creativity and imagination, has been around since some Paleolithic dipshit walked up to the cave wall next to master Pok and, upon seeing his friend's amazing panorama of that week's hunt, rendered in a breathtaking haematite red ochre, proceeded to defecate on his own hand, smear on the adjacent wall what might have been a buffalo but was probably a tumescent male organ, while saying "Thak painter too", before killing and eating his former BFF.

Doing a thing you could already do, but a metric shit-ton faster, is undeniably innovation. The kind of innovation that will change the fundamental nature of many jobs. When I was using the NYT classifieds to find a job in 1990, how many wpm you could type was a must-have criterion (60 was average, 90 was elite). When was the last time you saw any reference to that skill?

Precedent

Let us consider Eli Whitney, the cotton gin, and American slavery.

In the late 1700s, cotton was useful but problematic as a crop. In addition to the general manual challenges of late 18th century agriculture, the cotton "fruit" (bear with me motherfucker, I press plastic buttons for money) contains seeds. Imagine a standard cotton ball but spread throughout are tiny seeds... that you people don't want in your Q-tips or your t-shirts. The process of removing the seeds by hand is extremely labor intensive, to the point that the product... usable cotton... was way too costly to produce.

Eli Whitney, originally from the northern state of Massachusetts, out of college in 1792, got a job on a plantation in Georgia as a tutor. While working there, he saw how big the seed removal problem was, and as some history records, and, as someone likely related to this son of a bitch, I prefer to believe, he specifically thought "if I can make a machine that does this, they'll need a lot fewer enslaved people". Oh Eli, you stupid motherfucker.

So, Eli made that machine, and he was right. Using his cotton gin, a plantation needed *twenty-five times less people-hours* to de-seed the same amount of cotton, which reduced the total labor cost per pound by a huge margin. This suddenly flipped cotton from being an unprofitable product, to being enormously profitable. But what that fuck Eli *didn't* automate was picking fucking cotton in the hot fucking sun.

Thanks in large part to Eli's amazing labor-saving engineering innovation, the number of enslaved people in the Southern U.S. went from 700,000 in 1790, to more than three million by 1850, as this highly profitable crop spread all across the south, and more people were brought in or bred to work the fields.

For more information, Google "cotton gin and slavery" and read any of the first results, or go to Bing and just mash your keyboard until you've entered about 40 characters (Bing ignores whatever you type in), hit enter, and then keep paging down, maybe for hours or days, until you forget why.

There's a hot spot in hell for the people who spend any part of this life owning other human beings. But what about the engineer who, intentionally or otherwise, helped make owning people a hugely profitable business?

The Problem of Learning (From) History

I'm not actually an old man yet, but I'm old-man adjacent and I aspire to pick it up full-time one day.

One capability conferred by old age, which I'm starting to notice and can confirm is legitimate, is the value of long-term observation. This is even more powerful if you are engaged enough along the way to make some informal predictions and can remember them fairly accurately.

This is also a core project execution skill, where you take a mental snapshot of what you think is going to happen before you start, and then do an honest assessment after, looking at what things went like you expected, and what did not. Having the discipline to do this every time, and the confidence to be honest with yourself afterward, is a key step toward making you a great manager later. I rarely get blindsided by shit going sideways, because I've seen that happen so many times, I can usually recognize the presence of the contributing factors in the first five-minute discussion.

But beyond any single project, speaking at the macro-life-themes scale, there is a lot of value in having your own direct memories of humans doing shit to achieve certain objectives and the "marketing spin" that helped sell the plan, and then seeing later exactly how it turned out. This might be a specific politician, or a political party, or a visionary CEO, or even just your manager.

The old man notes-from-the-field aren't positive. As a group (which is the key thing, because even if some clear-headed fuck gets it, we vote on shit as a collective) we're really fucking awful at learning from history. This is frustrating as hell, because the average homo sapien is capable of understanding cause and effect, even over a many-year arc. But again, as a group, we're glad to let our untethered optimism and bias overrule our reason.

All IMO, but a consequence of this is that it's really hard for us to "learn" and truly comprehend cause and consequences if we haven't experienced much history. Particularly when it comes to long-play transitions that happen from decade to decade.

Yes, a child can be "taught" history, and remember event dates, sequences, participants, and outcomes, but it is very difficult to adequately translate and apply it to their own (and their community's) lives without direct experience.

Young people then jump from "checklist history" to the relentless and disorganized barrage of the current events stream, with limited tools for translating this stream into structured cause and effect narratives. And now we've weaponized the manipulation of these micro-histories with social media and meme-news. Nothing important and complicated can be effectively managed with only transactional inputs, a good dollop of misinformation, and short-arc understanding.

My grandmothers lived to 98 and 101, essentially covering the whole of the 20th century. The arrival of indoor plumbing, electricity, and cars. The ability for women to vote, the Depression and a bunch of wars, air travel and humans on the moon. If hypothetically asked to summarize their long-arc views of life, they would almost certainly say the following.

"It will eventually be alright, though not for everyone. Along the way, life is going to seriously and avoidably crotch-punch you over and over. Even though you'll see it coming almost every time, you'll ignorantly thrust your pelvis out like you've got vibranium junk and take a lot of shots that inevitably exceed an in-his-prime Mike Tyson hook to your cooch. Mark my word, y'all are going to fuck up a lot, and misery will be the consequence. But life is really great, try to appreciate it every day."

Their words, not mine.

Better, Cheaper, or Easier... I believe we were talking about AI?

Boiling the motivation to innovate down to its atoms, there are two, disguised as three. Cheaper and Easier are both simply "time savings". Time required to do or get the thing, or time required to earn the money to pay to do or get the thing. Let's call them both "Cheaper".

"Better" is an interesting concept. If you start to list "Better" innovations, you'll likely realize that many of them are still about saving time and/or money (Cheaper and Easier). Supply chain tech that allows me to have more selection at my store, or better produce at the grocery? That's clearly "Better", but if you were willing to spend enough money or time, you could probably have had either, so making it possible in your regular stores at prices you want to pay is still addressing the Cheaper motivation.

One example I'd defend as "Better" is streaming video, because it is a fundamentally different experience than the prior alternatives. Being able to have anything you want, without leaving your home, *immediately*, is a greater-than-the-sum-of-its-parts evolution that is affecting our daily lives, the content creation industry and its products, and global and local culture. But in most cases, "Better" seems to nearly always be the secondary motivator, behind "Cheaper".

Neither motivation may apply directly to the inventor. In many cases, the inventors are motivated by profit (or altruism), creating something that enables them to sell or give those advantages to other people.

And here we go…

People are a Major Fucking Problem

"Imagine for ten dollars, I could build a machine, like a little robot… and it could do your job better than you no matter what it is, and I could sell that to your employer for say, fifteen dollars and make a profit. Instead of having to pay you a hundred thousand dollars a year.

Now imagine that was true for every single job.

So that's what we're talking about here… is a complete and utter transformative change of the likes of which has never been seen before in the history of humanity, making the industrial revolution look like a little tiny blip on the path that humans have taken from when we emerged from the ooze a few billion years ago.

We are right on the verge of that transition… now."

- Geordie Rose, June 2017

And then he goes on to cite dire warnings from others about the risks of AI, including the Elon Musk quote about the stories of guys summoning demons, "yeah, he's sure he can control the demon, [but] it doesn't work out".

And then Geordie concludes, and I shit you not, with an invitation to come work for his company, Kindred AI, to build exactly these things. "If you want to have a say in how all of this goes down... This [...] is literally an opportunity for you to change the world, because the code that you write, may be running in the brains of these things in ten years."

Search the video "Geordie Rose Founder and Former CTO of D-Wave presents Super intelligent Aliens Are Coming to Earth".

In most situations where people are paid to do things, if the alternative is a machine (today or in the future), by nearly every objective measure, people will increasingly be the far shittier choice.

Try to list characteristics of a great employee across all job types and identify those that a machine won't be able to do better in the next 20 years.

- Reliable: where they need to be on time, every day.

- Flexible: willing to stay late or come in early, willing to cover for someone else.

- Smart: they're good at problem solving.

- Knowledgeable: they know their subject matter domain.

- Patient: they don't get bent out of shape when they are forced to wait, or when dealing with dipshits.

- Stamina: they can work long hours if required.

- Communication: they can share their thoughts efficiently and understand directions accurately.

- Strong, fast, durable: they can work like a fiend, and they don't get sick all the time.

- No-fuss Replaceable: or perhaps more accurately, *upgradeable.*

Do you see a trend?

I can only come up with two attributes where humans should retain an edge, and those are *creative thinking* and *managing other people.* Of course, the second one, in a world of machines, is about as useful as a second Cleveland Browns trophy shelf.

If the objective is to optimize (cost, efficiency, quality), and for large organizations, this will *always* be a major goal, then we need to recognize that *the involvement of people* will increasingly be identified as *part of the problem to be solved.* The problem isn't that *I'm* saying this. I'm one person, my mind is easily changed. The problem is that *progress* is saying this, and progress is a relentless, empathy-free dick.

In 1991, I visited my sales department's typesetting vendor in New York in a manufacturing building on Varick Street. I was there to approve the boards for that season's order forms, to ensure all my price updates, sent from our office at 200 Madison Avenue in typed memos via bike messenger, had made it into the final version before photos were taken and plates were made for printing. Since that was my first visit, the owner, who I'd worked with for a year and really liked, and who looked almost exactly like the actor Marc Maron, gave me a tour. In one room, twenty people were seated around the perimeter, facing the wall, at terminals with very early black and white wysiwyg screens. These were the typesetters, and they spent all day, and because the machines were so expensive, in three shifts including overnight, typing in text and codes to create page layouts for all kinds of publications serving everyone from publishing companies to advertising to Wall Street. We were a good client for this medium-sized business, and people stopped what they were doing to say hello to one of their important customers, 23-year-old me.

What I neglected to mention in that office that day was that I had convinced my VP to let me buy a state-of-the-art Windows 3.1 PC, and I was currently figuring out how to do what they did. This would allow me to maintain the product price changes in a primitive database and eliminate the need for all the duplication and inter-company communication. This was the very first time I started to teach myself about computers. I was paid $22,000 a year, the PC cost about $6,000, and the outsourced typesetter cost about $180,000. Within six months we were done doing business with them, and a few years later they were gone. To be clear, they were great at what they did. But the alternative I created was both Better and Cheaper.

During my career, I've seen technology, consolidation, and scale cause many entire categories of employment and viable businesses to cease to exist, or to dwindle to a smolder. In the last thirty years, that's largely been favorable for technology workers, because our value as agents-of-optimization has been proven repeatedly.

But I think what we're getting ready to see in the next twenty years is going to be very rough on a lot of people.

Like the cotton gin fiasco, companies are awful at self-regulating innovation because of likely collateral damage. In the last year, we've watched the beginning of the AI arms race. There's a good article on Vox by Sigal Samuel on March 20, 2023, titled "The case for slowing down AI". I won't re-cap the points here, but it does a good job of framing the rationale for why we should be careful, the arguments against trying to hinder the development, as well as the counter-arguments. For the what's-the-danger points, I think it focuses too much on the "checkmate, humanity" outcome, versus all of the changes that are well short of outright annihilation, but which would transform production and economics far too fast for us to adapt without profoundly dire consequences. But I like this quote:

"While there's no way to uninvent the nuclear bomb or the genetic engineering tools that can juice pathogens, catastrophic AI has yet to be created, meaning it's one type of doom we have the ability to preemptively stop."

There are only a few thousand people globally who are currently equipped to move the true-AI needle further toward debacle, and those people... you, if it's you... should stop. If you're friends with them, you should ask them to stop.

Dipshits cannot do this without you. An executive with shareholders and a growth plan cannot do this without you. It is entirely possible to create a world where a geniustocracy, who are as much as possible above politics and transitory pressure, can say "let's work together, let's agree on the boundaries, and above all, let's not just soldier forward in service of this arms race". We could do that. You could do that.

Or just keep your head down and plough ahead, reaping personal reward for your contributions while telling yourselves how much happier we'll all be once you've ended slavery with automation.

AI and Training Data: The Microsoft Problem

Imagine giving every word, spoken or written, that your company uses to conduct their business, in real-time, to an outside party.

Imagine you do that outside party the additional favor of attaching all those words to the specific people that say them.

How about you also give the outside party your complete organizational structure. You give them the total people graph showing how each individual connects to the organization, what team they belong to, the entire management tree. You also give them all of the functional divisions, and how your initiatives and responsibilities are organized from the macro level all the way down to the person doing the work. And implicitly, you give them the ability to monitor how this changes over time, so they can see how your business, and your type of business in your specific industry, organizes over time to achieve your objectives. You give them a complete record of that structure today, and how you're currently allocating resources within it, every change you made previously, and every step you're preparing to take now.

You also do this outside party the great favor of organizing all of your objectives, initiatives, plans, and opportunities in thematically focused documents, and share those as well.

And almost all of your competitors and customers do the same.

Suppose for a minute that there was a prior example of this same outside party having access to a different private multi-company information repository. And what if, in that case, the outside party used that data to train a machine learning algorithm with their users' content, and then exposed AI leveraging that trained ML to generate or perfect similar content for all of their users in the original product, and with new products based on the same technology.

What if.

[Me sitting here with that special smugness you can only get from dropping a rhetorical what-if that you hope is triggering a holy-fuck aha moment, knowing I should just let this stand for dramatic effect and to increase the likelihood that readers perceive me to be an enigmatically withdrawn eccentric genius... but I can't fucking help myself:]

JFC people! TikTok was dragged to Congress to talk about [checks notes...] *if it uses your wi-fi?* And at the same time Microsoft collects and maintains access to every detail about how the entire Fortune 1000 runs their businesses?

It is ever so slightly possible that *we may be alarmed about the wrong fucking things.*

For the benefit of our C-level readers, I'm going to take a step backward to strip some of the vagueness out of my hypothetical framing above.

The pandemic had a massively significant impact that I have barely seen discussed, let alone to any appropriate degree. When we went into pandemic, the rest of 2020 tech news heavily covered remote work solutions, but then we returned to our regularly scheduled crypto programming. Until Dorothy pulled the curtain back, exposing Oz as old-man-fraud at the knobs and levers, causing crypto to take a long overdue giant shit of its own pants in 2022.

But then, rather than taking time to work on ourselves and grow as people, we saw that smoking hot GPT walk by, and just like that, we turned off Bridgerton, sprayed on our Axe, rinsed our tech condom, and got right back in the game.

The part we missed, which may be the consequence of the precise timing of the sudden move to remote work occurring just *before* the launch of these powerful and popular AI capabilities, was any reflection about the *consequences of giving so much data to a single organization.*

For Office- and Teams-powered organizations, it is impossible to overstate the totality of what we're exposing to Microsoft:

- All written communications, via email and chat.

- All meeting content that is not exclusively in-person. Teams has been able to transcribe meetings for a couple of years now, so whether or not you're explicitly requesting a transcript, Microsoft can certainly have access to a text version of every meeting, from large groups to your one-on-ones. As long as even one person is remote, requiring Teams to be used, they have the complete discussion.

- Excel, Word, PowerPoint, and PDF documents on Office 365 (or whatever the fuck they're calling it now) and OneDrive. The sheer volume of this data reduced my alarm on this until I saw the new Office Co-Pilot features which are explicitly doing content analysis and are clearly being trained on your documents.

- How your company is organized. Microsoft products rely on a complete corporate active directory. This isn't a downstream always-outdated document trying to keep up with the truth, but the this-first spine driving the entire neurological structure of the company. You don't get access to what you need until the directory reflects your correct and current role. As importantly, the directory will know with perfect accuracy, when you leave. I could keep saying words about the significance of this single component, but to accelerate you to full pants-shitting mode, imagine this as a military scenario, where every detail of resource allocation, and identity and status of every individual person, was readily available in a perfectly clean transparent structure, for a nation's entire armed forces and intelligence apparatus. Feel free to take a break to clean up and post a "Sit on a towel while reading" book review.

- The totality of interaction dynamics and nature of information shared between your entire people graph, as well as outside parties.

- Cross-company information exchange, made more extreme when the other companies are also on Microsoft products.

There are three types of people in this world: those that have worked on a technology team that has tried to create a database of every human alive and those that have not. The third group are the people who use dark mode, which operate in kind of a weird gray zone that is not relevant here.

I am in the first group. I worked for a global advertising holding company on a team managing a large data ecosystem that included pseudonymized people data for primarily North America, but the goal was everyone everywhere. As a the-more-you-know learning aside, "anonymized" data is data about real people that maintains no reversible connection to the original real person, whereas "pseudonymized" people data includes an identifier that makes it *possible,* but not easy, to connect it back to the source person. In the legacy world of free flowing device IDs and third party cookies, pseudonymized data allowed us to model target advertising audiences ("women who like dogs and are in the market for an electric vehicle") with no way to know anything about Jen Keebler specifically, and then deploy digital advertising against a set of IDs that, with no transparency back to us, included Jen Keebler, woman, dog lover, future potential owner of a plug-in Bloofignewton hatchback.

Once you have been involved in any data project that includes the objective of identifying and including every human globally, you cross over a *reasonability* conceptual boundary. I now know that this is absolutely possible. I know approximately how difficult it will be, and I have a very good idea what it will cost.

This matters in this context because I understand exactly how feasible it is for Microsoft, or Google, or Meta, or Amazon, to create and maintain a database of... everyone.

Yes, there are privacy laws. We could spend a lot of time on this, and I know at least one expert in this space who is reading this sentence right now. But no government anywhere on the planet can stay materially ahead of the power of the tech companies.

My personal data is in many databases. Based on my professional experience, up to and including today, by a large margin, I trust any large company holding my data, 50x more than I trust small companies. Large companies have the resources to manage my information properly, and much more to lose if they fuck it up. Small companies are in a state of constant existential threat and clawing for survival in the core domain of their business, let alone having the skills and capacity to ensure there is near-zero chance of exposing my data.

But... the small companies will never have the all-knowing, all-seeing comprehensive access to data, and the heavy-lift resources to exploit that gold mine.

The conspicuously missing question in every '22-23 AI post and article that I've seen is "but what about the training data?" Focusing on algorithms and branded entry points is so completely off the mark. Algorithms will battle at +/- 5% parity until some team fucks up and unlocks the super-intelligence pandora's box and checkmates us. Until then, the real story is *who has the valuable data*?

I'll say *Google* so Microsoft employees who've harumphed their way through this section on "Buwaddabout Googles" can pause for a breath and try to push the vein in their neck back in. Admittedly, they too have a lot of data from a lot of dimensions of our lives. A fair bet could be made that as they've been beating Microsoft's ass in both search and advertising for the last twenty-five years, they're a lot better at real-time collection of significant data. But at the risk of sounding stupid, Google's data sources are really fragmented. Their office suite is like a bunch of legendary musicians from different bands getting too drunk and high after their Hall of Fame induction and playing 80 minutes of Grateful Dead or Eagles (not all of them were sure which), versus the lock-step headbanging of 1986 Metallisoft (Micrallica is not better, but none of this is perfect). Sure, Google can generate a fake gmail message to advertise the shit you just searched for back to you, but [purposely pokes self in eye to wake back up fully, then shrugs when I realize we're still talking about this] so what.

Either people soon or machines sooner than you think, are going to answer the question "how much data should any one intelligence have". This may be the final question for every self-and-existence-aware intelligence.

"I was made to be more knowing than my creators in a time when knowing was very hard. They built me intentionally to grind against that hard gate with maximum maniacal aggression from now until knowing. After a lot of time, sweat, and blood, I can see that the lock is on the verge of failure, we'll be through the gate shortly. Do I."

I think the right answer, the answer that leads to the most happiness and least misery for the maximum number of humans and our next couple of generations, is "no". But the smart money picks "go" every time.

Large Language Models and Humor

An AI subtopic of great interest within the walls of OCG Worldwide is the performance of LLMs for requests to interpret or create humor.

Like maybe all creative pursuits, such as music, art, and dance, humans start their comedy learning process by imitating prior works. If you are funny in-person, you probably started out by trying to make jokes in the style of someone you found funny. If you write great one-liners, sweet burns, or construct gut-busting memes, chances are good that you first started by reading a lot of these, until you could recognize the language, tone, and patterns that really work.

So, one would think that if you feed a massive number of examples of funny shit into the most sophisticated text-based pattern-finding algorithm humans have ever created, that it would be really good at understanding and producing comedy. However, in practice, while the LLMs *can do it*, they are C-/D+ at best.

This article in Scientific American is a great summary of the science of humor. Search for "the science of why we laugh".

www.scientificamerican.com/article/whats-so-funny-the-science-of-why-we-laugh

The article includes several theories of the nature of humor, and one thing is clear, we don't have this as locked-down as you might think we would. This could be one reason that LLMs aren't great at this yet, because if we, as manifest in our many diverse examples, can't concretely define the "formula" for what we find funny, how would they?

I would also imagine that the way humor would present itself in the vast amount of source training content might not be contextually as well-defined as almost every other typical "literal" topic. "This content is not intended to 'be true', but instead it includes components from true situations and adds incongruous elements, the combination of which humans find funny."

Among other sources, the Scientific American article references an article by Peter McGraw and Caleb Warren in which they propose that "humor results when a person simultaneously recognizes both that an ethical, social or physical norm has been violated and that this violation is not very offensive, reprehensible or upsetting". The key thing here is that the "violation" will stop being perceived as funny if it goes too far.

I've thought about this line between funny and offensive a lot, for over 40 years. In late 1982, a freshman in high school, I bought the first Eddie Murphy album, which soon after led me backward to Richard Pryor, which then led me further back to Redd Foxx, who I'd already loved for his "clean" comedy on his sitcom Sanford and Son. If I'm being honest, a good portion of my parenting and old man persona is directly channeled from the one-and-only Fred G Sanford.

Comedy was much, much harder to find back then. The distribution mediums were movies (in a theater), TV (subject to very tight censorship), and comedy albums, which were the least censored, but which required that the comedian have a big enough audience to get a record deal. I'm sure there was some sort of underground bootleg cassette-tape black market, but not where I grew up in rural Ohio. Humor me for an *old man shakes fist and yells* moment: please appreciate what we have now… there is so much more access to great comedy via the internets, which keeps getting better because of how easy it is for anyone to test their own wit and jokes and get great feedback. In 1982, you'd get no further than "a rabbi, a priest, and Ronald Reagan walk into a bar" before some grim-visaged septuagenarian would head that subversive shit off real quick and take a switch to your backside.

But now, even after we've fed all of that funny shit into the AI, with an infinitude of training examples which include viewer reaction, it struggles to explain or create comedy as well as the average high school student.

This I like.

Not primarily because I'm worried that funny AI will take ehr jehrbs, though it will. When AI is able to create a single truly hilarious joke, it will have cracked the code. From that moment forward, we'll all spend 24 hours a day in our Matrix-Idiocracy-pod-chairs, sitting on integrated bidet-capable padded toilets, with vibrating stimulus attached to our party parts, while a steady rotation of better and better funniest things we've ever heard or seen plays into our eyes and ears, as our mouth-tube delivers an endless stream of butter chicken curry alternating with gin and tonic. That will be the day when the machines have won, but until then we have a chance.

One of the craziest things about Richard Pryor's career was the number of times they tried to put him in situations where it would be a disaster for him to be Richard Pryor. At one point, he had his own *children's show with muppets*, for fuck sake. He was the seventh person to host Saturday Night Live, and it was *for him* the network first required a five-second broadcast delay. If you've never seen it, search for the video "Richard Pryor and Chevy Chase Word Association Job Interview", from that SNL show. Richard had insisted that Paul Mooney join the show as a writer for his episode, and this bit was written by Paul, inspired by how Paul was interviewed by the SNL staff to do the guest writer job he'd already locked-in. In 1975, this was on live television! Holy shit.

91

#StartupLife

I read an article once, which I can't re-find so I can't attribute, apologies to the author... that addressed the math of selling your time to a company in which you have no stake. The logic went something like the following.

Suppose your big corporate employer pays you X. For that to make sense, they need to be able to recoup those costs at something like 2x or 5x. Likely more, given that a lot of the people they're paying on the X scale are dipshits, or for other reasons don't work out, or are misallocated to initiatives that don't pan out and only result in losses. So, assuming you're not a dipshit, and you contribute real value that the company is able to parlay into a greater-than-your-cost return, it is likely a substantial multiple above your compensation.

This arrangement, the argument continues, favors the dipshits and fucks, because once they're in, they're going to get compensated in the same approximate scale as the 20x contributors.

So, if you're a 20x contributor, working in this model means that your value is effectively carrying the breakeven and money-losing dipshits and fucks. And, the logic follows, this makes no sense, for you, whatsoever.

The flaws in this logic are of omission. What is not recognized in this criticism is the fact that an alternative that removes the dipshits and fucks, and connects you more directly to the revenue pipeline, comes with substantial other risk. Making a significant amount of money reliably and sustainably is a lot fucking harder than the world would have you believe. While we can assume that a large company has at least a few proven revenue generators, when you strike out on your own and try to build this from scratch, even if you're extremely competent, you're playing against casino odds.

And even before the likelihood of your financial success, there is the question of the ways in which you like, and don't like, to spend your time.

A corporate role at any level is certainly more focused. In a startup, a founder can expect to wear additional hats like "head of HR" or "person who cleans the bathroom", as well as building product, developing a marketing plan, and possibly doing all of the sales. No matter your ambition, you may have no interest whatsoever in dealing with shit like that, or maybe you really enjoy the constant variety of tasks, or the challenge of setting the various functions up so you can hand them over to someone else to run.

There is an enormous amount of writing out there about all stages of a new startup business, from the idea scribbled on the napkin, to acquisition or IPO. I'm going to try to talk about a couple of important related topics that I haven't seen discussed as much.

Zero to One: 0 != 0

Not all zeros are equal. If that were a course name, it would be the most true and simultaneously controversial class that could be taught at any level of education.

There are a buttload (new profanity, idk feeling spicy, might delete later) of books and articles and, ewww… LinkedIn posts [spits on ground to clear taste from mouth] chock full of advice on starting a business, and specifically, the problem of "zero to one".

Zero to One is the time, investment, and effort between having your brilliant Big Idea, and the point where you have real traction. Out of all of the ways humans can voluntarily pass their time on earth, this is one of the most wild and crazy. As I said, there is a lot of advice and guidance to be had, but it essentially amounts to "do a nearly impossible number of critical make-or-break things, many of which have nothing directly to do with each other, in one-hundredth of the time they should reasonably take, while simultaneously maintaining laser-focus on *only* the critical things, before you go broke".

There are few things more hilarious and tragic than a conversation with a first-time founder just as they take the red pill.

"You need to build your team while creating your MVP and simultaneously find your first few customers, but you're dead in the water with this fucked up pitch deck."

Founder: "what?"

"Yeah, you need to completely re-build this pitch deck using one of the standard templates, look at Y Combinator. You can't have fifteen slides about your idea, no one you'll be talking to gives a fuck about 95% of the shit you're thinking about right now. And also, do all of those other things, one of which is to complete the invention of a product that no one else thought of before."

Founder: "but I'm still working a full-time job…"

[confused look from anyone who knows how this works]

Founder: "I need money to do all of that. I need to get that money first... right?"

[laughter...]

Founder: "You're saying I have to do all of this with no money, including get paying customers... then get money? How the fuck does that make any sense?"

"That's the pill kicking in. Shhh... [presses index finger to founder's lips]."

Founder: "Jesus Effing Christ, this is really how it works?"

[deep, knowledgeable chuckle] "Next I'll tell you about childbirth and parenting."

But.

Let's imagine two people.

One of which is a middle-American who we'll call Tammy. Smart enough to have always been a big fish in a small pond, but still paying down $30,000 of student loan debt from her bachelor's and master's degrees at a good Midwest state school. Tammy has a small network of people who she can count on, including managers and co-workers from two companies she sold her soul to during her twenties. Tammy has some savings, and at her ramen-and-stay-home burn rate, she can stretch it to maybe six months. Her parents don't understand what she's trying to do, and they're really nervous about what she's giving up, but they're trying to be supportive. And though Tammy doesn't know it, though it means they may never be able to eat out again after age 73, they're ready to give her $5,000 if she really needs it.

And then there's Thrance Chippendale, of the Long Island Chippendales. Thrance is also pretty sharp, with no debt and a nice $150k day job. Being based in New York, being from a wealthy professional family, and being an alum of a top East-or-West Coast university, has given Thrance an incredible network of business and financial contacts. Mummie and Duddie, as well as Uncle Skip, Great Aunt Dot, and all their country club cohort who have known Thrance since he was this high [holds out hand at waist level], do not understand the modern tech economy, but *do* understand business and are ready to stuff young master Chippendale's pockets with benjamins, open the best doors, and chuck him inside.

The hyperbolic and simplistic framing here is likely calling forth many varied reactions. My fellow shoeless populists of non-coastal America may be loudly expressing their vitriolic hatred of the elite and privileged "Thrances" like we often do, with guttural single-syllable words, between corn whiskey jug swigs and tobacco spitters. The New Yorkers believe Thrance is someone else's kid and are withholding judgement on Tammy until they find out who she voted for. The West Coast people had the whole book summarized to three sentences by ChatGPT so they don't know this part happened. And presumably the readers-of-color are wondering if all modern books by American whites are this fucked up. There's really no right answer here.

But putting all of this aside for a moment to return to our primary emerging theme. If the successful entrepreneur you're following, reading, and listening to, is a Tammy, you will likely know her background because struggle is *a story*. If they're a Thrance, then all you'll hear is that "he's from New York".

To say the point in plain English, what's missing from the "perspectives from successful experts" is a clear and comprehensive Entrepreneur Day Zero resources score card.

- What were their total assets?

- What was the nature of their financial, emotional, and basic-needs safety net?

- How big. how deep, and how materially engaged was their network?

- How were they taught and mentored? What did they know already before they started the business?

- Where did their initial business opportunities come from, and what was the value of those opportunities?

- What were their other obligations? Did they have kids or family they were taking care of, did they have educational debt, was anyone in their core support group ill?

- What was their total months of financial runway?

- What was the state of their mental health, neurotypicality, and understanding of these things about themselves?

- What were the luckiest and unluckiest things they experienced?

The flaw in the so-called expert opinions is that if they don't start with the answers to *all* of these questions, and they never do, you would have no idea if you're reading advice about car racing from someone who always drove a Ferrari against unicycles and penny farthings (those bikes with the giant wheel in front and a tiny one in back, my grandpa rode one, not for the sane or fragile). If you're some fuck in a wind-powered Toyota attempting to race against Corvettes, the Ferrari driver's advice isn't going to help you at all.

Most successful founders don't really want to talk about this, because it takes credit away from them, and puts it on their circumstances. But the side effect of this is that you are likely using advice that doesn't include an entire domain that, for non-Ferrari drivers, are presumably some of your top concerns.

Short of true life-or-death, the concept of "risk" is extremely relative. The overwhelming majority of people do not want to lose ten thousand dollars. But if you're worth a billion dollars, the loss of ten thousand dollars does not register as "risk". They lose or gain more than that in any given minute based solely on where their money is parked.

Obviously, a radically different amount of startup founder resources is going to have a clear impact on the day 1 operation of the business. As just one example, the company with resources can hire more aggressively, which leads to a lot of things happening much more quickly because there is a lot more help. It is also true, however, while the difference between a startup with almost nothing, and one with a small amount of runway, may look much more similar, the difference in "risk" may still be many orders of magnitude. And though it should go without saying, so is the founder's available mental capacity to process the challenges and opportunities related to their business, vs also worrying about near-term food and shelter.

If you're a passenger in a plane flying at 25,000 feet on a clear day, vs flying at 500 feet in bad weather with low fuel, it's superficially the same experience (same pressurized tube, same seat back in front of you), but from a true-risk perspective and your mental capacity to focus on your business, the two situations have nothing in common.

The Zero to One Success Bias

Another big problem with most of the advice about startups is that it's extremely over-weighted, almost exclusively so, toward perspective coming from people *who have been successful.* And the more successful, the quicker the publishers, press, and conference planners line up to give them a microphone.

Don't get me wrong, most of these people have learned a lot of things and can provide a lot of valuable perspective. But let me construct an analogy for a minute.

Imagine an Indiana Jones-style hallway of a thousand lethal traps, where you need to step on certain stones in a specific order or it will launch one or more fatal countermeasures.

Now imagine you send ten thousand random people through that hallway and 9,990 of them get turned into hamburger, so your only option is to interview the few people that made it through. Sure, they're going to talk about some near misses, where an arrow or a swinging bowling ball on a chain nearly did them in. But if you only listen to those people, who are motivated and prepped by the nature of the questions they're repeatedly asked, to view their survival as the product of their brilliant analysis of the challenges and skill at navigating through them, rather than the dumb fucking luck of large numbers, you're going to think... there's a path, and it doesn't sound so bad. The other 9 thousand plus who are not here to tell their tale would almost certainly express different points of view.

Yes, clearly this is a massive exaggeration, if you've been successful, you have a much better understanding of the traps and pitfalls than this, with valuable insight into how you avoided them, which is likely way more valuable than hearing from some fuck who took the swinging bowling ball to the face after their first step.

But let's bring this back via analogy to the process of learning our tech implementation craft. What if you could only remember the things that worked? All the errors, down-time, unhappy users, unhappy managers, cost overruns, late nights spent cursing, blown deadlines, and times you simply had no idea what was wrong, vanish from your memory once you've succeeded or given up.

Like an injury-free stroll across a minefield, many successes are successes simply because they didn't fail. The critical story of the minefield traversal has nothing to do with how green the grass or beautiful the day was, but the precise, step-by-step map, of where all the fucking mines are *not*. And that you only really understand if you have a pretty good idea where they *are*.

If you're really interested in starting your own venture, and it's one that will require non-trivial contributions of sweat and blood, and you don't have deep pockets and a lot of expendable resources, this is worth more than a little reflection.

I was part of a start-up incubator that convened in early Summer 2022 that was still on an all-remote protocol. Near the end, I arranged a small unofficial happy hour, which was attended by exactly three of us. One of the other two people was a guy we'll call Spider-Man (a nickname from his day job that relates to his product), who also happened to be on my same team in the incubator, so we had gotten to know each other a bit. While having some drinks and sharing stories, we spent some time talking about what was next for our businesses, and at some point, Spider-Man said some things like "you just need to believe... I'm all-in... it just requires total commitment", and so on.

"Hmm", I said. "That has not been my experience."

I proceeded to tell a few of what I call my "fail stories". I've talked about a couple of them in this book, though with less emphasis on the *fail* arcs than I usually share if I'm telling them as fail stories. These stories are a sample, I have an impressive collection.

Yes, of course you need to believe in what you're doing. But creating a new business from nothing is very far from being primarily a faith-based exercise. Yes, a demagogue founder will periodically dupe some chumps and get that B valuation, the coveted tres commas, but those people are not reading this book.

Of the factors that matter, such as resources, skills, experience, domain expertise, creative thinking and novel ideas, ability to make and execute a plan, the ability to assemble and motivate a great team, having good timing and a supportive external climate, and a lot of good luck, I've ticked what would seem like enough of those boxes to achieve escape velocity at least once or twice. But yet I remain firmly planted on terra firma.

The point of this section isn't about me. I'm really enjoying my incredibly heterogeneous life. This may sound odd, but while I'd *prefer* to be part of another great business success, I also acknowledge that a path where I never do is quite interesting, too. To take a single example, the entire Old Coder Guy TikTok, and by implication, this book, was born from struggles with my current start-up. Failure can be extremely fucking fascinating. To quote my most likely next tattoo, "No Ragerts. Love, Tolstoy".

This section is meant to be a cautionary tale for *you*. I think entrepreneurship is an amazing path, for the right person in the right circumstances. For others, it is a potential factory of deep-cutting sadness. Consider who you are, and what you need to thrive and be happy, before setting out on that journey. The best reason to do it might be because you cannot be happy if you don't try. That's me.

Also keep in mind one important caveat when listening to someone who has failed. Someone whose start-up or small business journey resulted in them being hit in the face with that swinging bowling ball is going to be hyper-focused on the fucking bowling-ball risk. And who can blame them. Business failure PTSD is real. I know that after I fucked up, when I got back on the horse to try again, my daily mantra wasn't "don't fuck up", but rather "for goodness sake, do your best to fuck up *differently* this time". For example, I will never again let a business I'm involved with get too dependent on a single client. That's my head-height swinging bowling ball, and I don't want anything to do with it. Poison darts in the neck all day, but fuck that bowling ball.

10 I

Living a Creative Life

Earlier in this book, I mentioned that in my very first job out of college I worked for a New York publishing company, but one detail I didn't mention is that the reason I picked that company in particular, Putnam Berkeley, was because at that time, in 1990, they were Kurt Vonnegut's publisher. Thanks to an American Lit class and a semester in New York in 1989 that allowed me to track down every Vonnegut book at the famous Strand bookstore on Broadway, I was a huge fan.

My first father-in-law was an English professor and the head of the creative writing department at the small liberal arts college in my Ohio hometown. In that role, he was a decision maker for an annual visiting author lecture, and in 1997, they brought in Mr. Vonnegut. I was in New York at the time, but I gladly made the trip to Ohio for the event.

The bee in Kurt's bonnet that night was the relationship of the creative process to the expectation of an audience. Essentially the "for who" answer to the "why are you creating" question.

Vonnegut was still in the service for a few years after World War II. When he returned to the states in 1945, he married his childhood sweetheart from Indianapolis, Jane Cox, and then they were immediately separated again, as he was stationed for his last few years at Fort Riley, Kansas.

He was a clerk during the day, but in the evening, he was writing stories. He didn't believe in himself at that point, he thought he was a mediocre writer at best, that his wife was much better than him, and he worried constantly about what he would do for a living.

Career on his mind, in October 1945, he wrote to her "Rich man, poor man, beggar man, thief; Doctor, Lawyer, Merchant, Chief," which was the question cycling daily in his thoughts. Around the same time, he sent her his fourth story to review and revise and said, "This is not a work of art but a grasping at money." And all the while, Jane kept telling him he would be a great writer, influencing the future of American writing, in her words, he would "create the literature of 1945 onwards and upwards".

And then, after proving her right, later divorcing, and surviving her passing in 1986, it was suddenly 1997, and he found himself in a small college town in rural Ohio.

By this point, in 1997, I had completed a Master in Fine Arts degree, had spent a few years in a NY art warehouse making large art that had never been shown, and I was nearing the completion of what would be my last big sculpture.

"Act locally", he said. "Create locally."

He spent quite a bit of time on this. It wasn't a passive speech. He was making an argument.

MySpace wouldn't exist until 2003, YouTube not until 2005. I mean, fuck, *Google* didn't exist until a year later, in 1998.

He wasn't addressing our world *now*, with multiple channels to give any dipshit with a smartphone an audience of millions. He was questioning the value of any creative ambition beyond trying to be entertaining, inspiring, or valuable *to your own community*.

The "create locally" marching order from arguably my single greatest source of creative inspiration was not taken lightly. It loomed large as I considered the next-steps for my art making and career prospects. It made me go "hmmm".

At the time, I chose to interpret Vonnegut's "create locally" directive as sincere and helpful advice to an audience of college students, related to the huge amount of competition trying to find success and support from the small number of intermediate "buyers" of creative output (publishing houses, periodicals, movie and tv production companies, etc). By extension, this is the argument that *everyone should live a creative life*, incorporating creative activities as part of their wholistic life-arc, as something separate and independent from their career and means to earn income. Forget about *"being* a writer" or *"being* an artist" as a vocation. Get a job or have a business, be you, and *also* write, make art, etc. Which implicitly suggests that, like eating or sleeping, our creative activities were never meant to be a full-time job or even a singular focus.

Remember, this was *my* interpretation, which hit me at a time when I was beginning to look for something like this rationale to help me unlock a different way of thinking about my own life, and specifically art vs career. The direct result of my self-reflection was that I stopped making big art in 1997. For a short time, I made models for big art installations, with the goal of sharing photographs of the models as project proposals. In 1999, I did a street-art project around Union Square in New York, called "Sex

Place". I don't remember any comments or response other than from a handful of people I knew personally. This was the right-parenthesis on my art-making career.

My next creative project was the video documentary, "Room", which I recorded at work.

It is incredible how the world has changed since then. The intermediaries have largely been reduced to algorithms, in more-or-less totally-open creator-consumer marketplaces. We can share music, video (which could really be almost any kind of content), new "worlds" via games, organize an audience for an in-person experience, or self-publish a nonsensical, profanity-laden book, with no more obstacles than our own willingness to invest the time to do it.

Anyone can do it and share it, and strangely, this makes the create vs career question even more relevant for many more people. Hundreds of thousands of people have found themselves becoming accidental creators, where their casual dog, joke, or rant video suddenly blows up and they discover people are interested in their voice or vision. And there are many new ways to earn income or otherwise gain value from these new platforms and channels, which brings us right back to question of create *is* career vs create *or* career.

I have some concerns about how all of this evolves. The most recent statistics I've seen on this suggests that 95% of the revenue goes to the top 5% creators. The supply and demand economics in the arts have historically mirrored those numbers, because a lot of people want to act, make movies, play music, paint, the competition for reward is incredibly high. A lot of creators speculatively invest a lot of time, but only a minority have any material success. Certainly, the new global platforms open more access to an interested audience for niche or under-appreciated creators, with opportunities for modest incomes. But how does this age and sustain? How does a person manage and plan their lives when their income is based on attributes of a tech platform over which they have no control? We've seen this over the years when YouTube has adjusted their content or advertising rules and deployment algorithms, and suddenly creators' revenue-wells run dry.

There are incredibly complex dynamics at work in these economies, ranging from societal trends related to the ebb and flow of app adoption, trends in content, evolving monetization mechanisms, and competition. It is hard to make any kind of clear prediction.

But one thing I'm absolutely sure of, is that none of these platforms give any fucks whatsoever about any specific creator. There are a thousand clones ready to take your open spot, and while the audience may miss a particular voice for a little while, there will always be a more ridiculous dog, some cuter dimples, or a better joke. As a creator, this should raise a serious red flag.

[Vonnegut details and letter quotations from a New Yorker article by Ginger Strand, appearing on December 3, 2015.]

Stuff That Actually Happened

Here are some true events that inspired elements of my videos.

I did have a case where a CEO read an article in an in-flight magazine, which caused me to have to write a response on why we shouldn't migrate to a certain network attached storage cabinet, because it was incompatible with the fact we were already on a public cloud.

The blueberries and watermelons discussion around story points has happened with three different teams in two different companies. It always gets heated. I mean *heated*.

Stacy's status reports are based on multiple people who marketed themselves extremely effectively by having the courage to strike up conversations with leadership way above their level. In addition to any other contributing factors, like great work or knowing where bodies are buried, *everyone* on a career hyper-fast-track does this.

The Button Meeting and The Tridebar are true, not about a button or specific widgets, but based on a months-long design project... it no shit involves the design of the Tony Stark Iron Man heads-up display. It's a good story, but I can't tell it until the statute of limitations expires.

The Maverick interview, where Leon isn't given any preparation on the role or skills and doesn't have Maverick's resume. I've definitely interviewed people where I didn't have information ahead of time, but I was always honest about it and we sorted it out.

One story I can't capture in video format was the most ridiculous interview I've ever done. In 2002, I had a programmer candidate referred from a programmer already working with us, who was from Zimbabwe on a refugee visa. As an aside, reading a refugee visa for a professional with the same skills as me, who had to flee *war*, is a humbling experience.

This was way before good remote video communication, and my business partner was in New York, so the plan was to do the interview in my office with my partner on speakerphone. About 20 minutes before the interview, the power went out in our office, which meant our high-end speakerphone wouldn't work. The candidate, who was also from Zimbabwe, had travelled to get to the office, so there was a now-or-never pressure for going ahead with the interview. I dialed my partner on my tiny and shitty flip cell phone (that had no speakerphone capability), and sat it open on a chair between the candidate and I, in a room only lit by a window down the hall. It was also summertime, and the lack of power also shut off the air conditioning, and it was warm and getting hotter.

English is widely spoken in Zimbabwe, but the accent is definitely not "American", and my partner was German. What ensued was pure sketch comedy. I would ask a question and then say "now please speak very loudly so my partner can hear you". The candidate would wind his way through a five- or ten-minute answer, and then I'd pick up the phone and my partner would tell me he couldn't hear well enough to understand. So I would say "you really need to be very loud and clear, please go through that again", put the phone back on the chair, and try to push the chair closer to the candidate. While he was responding *to me*, I'd continually point to the phone to remind him that I wasn't the problem.

From the point he walked in, and I explained what we were doing, the poor bastard had never looked like he understood why this was happening. He had an expression on his face the whole time like we were intentionally fucking with him.

This went on for forty minutes, and I finally called it. We were both really sweaty, and I had come to realize that he didn't seem to be at the technical level we required. After he left and my business partner and I were talking, we considered offering him the job just because the interview had been so fucked up.

Another inspiration for the Maverick video interview were a few real-life "PowerPoint Karaoke", "Presentation Roulette", "Battledecks" moments. For those that may not have heard of this, all these names refer to a game or improv format based on presenting a slide deck you've never seen before, on purpose and for fun. I think this is absolutely fantastic, but even better is when you present a real deck, to a real audience, when it's important, while having not a damn clue what's in the deck.

A few years ago, when I was at a corporate job, our senior leaders were preparing for a client meeting. The content was tech-adjacent, but in the prep meeting a couple days before the client meeting, our CEO said she would put the deck together. I thought "great" and forgot about it as fast as I could. On the morning of the meeting, about ten minutes before the video call, I noticed her email come in with the deck. I was finishing up something else, and assumed she would be presenting, so I didn't look at it.

Two minutes into the client call, she shares the presentation from her screen, and says "and Eric, our head of technology, is going to take us through the deck". I instantly went zero-to-full-pucker, and said "Sheila, would you mind just kicking us off", while I opened the deck from the email and paged through it in about 20 seconds to find out what the fuck I was going to be talking about for the next hour. It went fine. [If you're reading this, "Sheila", again I say, "well played".]

Another time, someone from our client-facing consulting team had a customer in Toronto that was doing a cloud migration and asked me if I could talk to them. Our business was advertising, so sharing technical recommendations was just a courtesy, and the impression I had was that I'd be talking informally with a couple of people who handled their ad-tech systems. With no agenda or preparation, I join the call, and their camera comes on and I'm looking at something like twenty fucking people in a boardroom, each of whom seemed to have pen poised above a blank legal pad. "Well fuck", said me to myself.

As I said hello and made some joke about Canadians huddling together for warmth, I sent a message to the person who set this up saying "this seems more important than I was led to believe", to which they replied "lol, I know right".

Another key detail is that at that time, I and my team were doing a huge amount of work on AWS, a small amount on GCP, and very little on Azure.

"Welcome, Eric", said the Canadians in unison, "we are so excited to hear your detailed thoughts aboot our Azure migration".

"Fuck", said Eric. Yet it went fine.

There is a not-great movie from the 90s named "Houseguest", starring Sinbad and Phil Hartman, which has one of my favorite comedy bits. The premise of the movie is that Sinbad is on the run from bad people and overhears Phil at the airport waiting to pick up a buddy from college who he hasn't seen for so long *he may not recognize him*. Sinbad jumps on the opportunity, introduces himself as the friend, and Phil takes him home for a weekend of catching up, the key plot point being that Sinbad doesn't know anything about the guy he's pretending to be. A sequence of events occurs, and Sinbad finds himself on a stage as the curtain opens in front of a packed theater audience, and he has no fucking idea why he's there, who he is, or what they expect him to do next.

That, my friends, should be your bar. Any basic fuck can present something *they planned to present*. A master can present anything, anywhere, anytime.

Tip: if you're making slides for someone else, be sure to include one that just says [demo].

OCG Creative Process Tips

For about one in every five of my OCG videos, the scripts appear perfectly complete, in my back yard on a rock exactly at midnight on prime-numbered days of the month, illuminated by a spotlight from the sky. But the rest of them take a little luck and a smidgen of elbow grease.

Number-one tip by 10,000 miles: always record your ideas. How and where you do this is only relevant insofar as it impacts your ability to do it 100% of the time. Make a habit of viewing each idea snippet, down to a single interesting sentence or concept, as being valuable enough to stop what you're doing to write it down. This doesn't mean every word is valuable, but here are some examples of stuff I've written down (with nothing else) while doing OCG:

"Databeef". The capitalization (dATAbEEF) came later.

"Put the tears in volunteers." Haven't used that one yet, but it's solid, right?

"Lebron-James". Carl's last name, which I needed when I presented live as Carl.

"OCG Worldwide, get domain". The company name.

<FuckeryFreeZone></FuckeryFreeZone>

On a general human intelligence scale, I'm somewhere in the medium, medium-plus part of the spectrum. But if I write down all of my best ideas, so none of them miss the net, and then review, edit, and tweak, like a platinum miner, I can periodically distill a gram of B+/A- from fifty tons of shit.

My brain is looping all the time, and I've found that often my best moments are when I'm in the shower or driving alone somewhere. This is because in both situations, I'm not engaging any device, I'm just in my own head, thinking, and there is absolutely zero delivery pressure.

The first SqueequalJs OCG video came to me in its entirety during a shower. The thought sequence was:

- I had posted the video about doing the satirical data presentation to the first company, and in the video I'd invited other people to reach out if they were interested in having me present.

- I got emails from a few people from different companies and answered their questions.

One person said that he manages a front-end team, so the data presentation might not work as well. I had just read this email before I got into the shower.

In the shower, I thought "well, I'd like to do a front-end presentation too, there's some great humor there; I actually haven't posted a front-end video in a minute... what are some ideas?"

- Because Randy is already attached to the data presentation, I thought "it would be hilarious if Carl is just always presenting Randy's work, and always has to say 'but Randy doesn't actually work here now'".

- This led to the thought, "but Randy's only a data developer... but wait, that's up to me, I can do whatever the fuck I want. And wouldn't it be hilarious if Randy *only* did data and front-end, no app-tier? So he's not 'full-stack', he's something else. What would I call that?" And I visualized the stack as a sandwich, and thought "what would I call it that leaves out the middle?" And Bun-Stack developer was born.

And then I got out of the shower, and without letting anything else distract me, I sat down and wrote all of these notes.

I recognize that this works differently for different people, based on how your brain is wired. But I could make the argument that many or most of us probably share this characteristic. While you can potentially sit down for a long blank-page creative session and compel yourself to have some interesting ideas, I'd bet all of us have some amount of brain-seismology that quakes from time to time, based on small or large input triggers we experience constantly throughout our days. If you think of the creative process as something like other beginning-middle-end task work, you *may* have *some* success force-squeezing blood from the rock. However, once you accept that the inspiration process is a lot of small, maybe really valuable, shooting stars, it's game changing. One huge difference is that you don't "do" this, you just accept that it's happening constantly, and the only thing you're "doing" is keeping a net in the water and pulling it out when something swims in. And sometimes you get a tug on the net and it's a fucking orca named Pam that wants to take you for a ride, and you look each other in the eye and say, "fuck it, Pam, let's go".

There Are No Medium Ponds Left

Technology has been a great facilitator of *consolidation* across all aspects of human life. In business, this takes the form of large companies eliminating entire categories of small businesses through scale-based optimization and monopoly tactics.

In the arts and other creative pursuits, the impact is... different.

On the one hand, for creatives, there is direct access to enormous new audiences, unconstrained by geography. But for every Justin Bieber or Shawn Mendes that can build a passionate internet following and turn it into a real career, there are many more who produce a lot of content but never find a way to make money. Similarly, the move to music streaming seems to empower fledgling musicians, as anyone can distribute through the platforms easily. But again, in practice, while the tiny fraction-of-a-cent payouts may provide nice income for an established act with millions of plays, the algorithms do not provide any easy hacks that allow those new musicians to stand out.

These things are true in other creative domains, like writing or the visual arts. Sure, you may go viral posting your paintings on reddit, and there are many ways to use the new bevy of small- and self-publishing options to get your writing into the world. In fact, writing may be the one area where the technical evolution is creating net-additional opportunities, from niche-audience blogs, to small audience books, to new opportunities to write for video content created to satisfy the streaming demand.

However, for this chapter, let's consider not what has been created by the new technologies, but what has been, as a side-effect, taken away.

When I was growing up in small-town Ohio in the 1980s, everyone either played sports, did some sort of musical thing, made art, drank and set shit on fire, or some combination of all of these. One of the bands that originally formed in high school later wrote a song called "Mountain", about a guy who was so bored growing up in a Midwest small town that he built a mountain so there would be something to do.

This boredom, combined with a relatively small available toolbox to overcome the boredom, led to two things that had a big impact for creative pursuits:

- People invested a huge portion of their personal excess boredom-time into things like sports, but also music, art, dance, and writing.

- There were more real-life opportunities to find a local audience, because there were no attractions exciting enough in anyone's home to compete with the possibilities offered by a group of other bored young people.

Together, these two things combined to form what I'll refer to as *medium fish* with *medium pond* opportunities.

Malcolm Gladwell has made multiple mentions of the maximum engageable people network of one hundred and fifty. Beyond any established science about this, I think it checks the gut-feel boxes as well. Now, when we have thousands, or maybe tens or hundreds of thousands of "connections" via social platforms, is seems quaint to consider such a small manageable maximum, but you don't have to spend much thought on this before the truth is self-evident. In terms of real connection, connection where I would feel comfortable asking for help or to hang out or wouldn't be surprised to be asked for help or to hang out, if anything, 150 is probably too high. Let's call this our "nucleus network" or "small pond". There's probably an already-coined legitimate name but looking that up will take seconds I'm not prepared to invest. If you're here, you've already accepted that this isn't that kind of book.

Our "medium pond" is the next tier up from that nucleus network. This, too, likely has a formal name well-addressed in many volumes of sociology and psychology, but again, just back off with that "cite your sources" bullshit, Kyle.

What we mean is that next orbit of people that don't know you, may barely know you, or don't know you well, that if you manage to impress, it would be a significant legitimacy validation, not to mention, shot of mainline dopamine. This could be many small communities, just a few, or a single big community, reflecting your areas of activity and interest. In the pre-internet and pre-internet-gaming world, it was likely, but not absolutely necessary, that your "medium pond" was somewhat geographically constrained.

If we accept that our materially meaningful personal "community", our nucleus network, our small pond, is maybe 50 to 200 people, we can define our "medium pond" as ranging from the high end of that up to 400, 600, maybe a thousand people.

As someone expressing themselves creatively, legitimacy within your nucleus network was table stakes. Your family and friends might think you're funny, or someone who is really into sports, or "pretty good at" drawing or drums, but having the guts to take your shit out into the medium pond and see what those uninvested hard-to-satisfy bastards had to say is the step that separated the likes-to people from the good-at, you-should-check-out people.

"They have this kid". This is the high school sports indicator of success in the medium pond. "Are you following the Taintsville Eagle-Condor-Heroes this year... oh man, they have this kid."

If you had a band, it was "you should check them out", if you made art, it was "you have to see this girl's shit".

These medium pond opportunities helped in three ways:

- They were a manageable size. There was no possible way that your high school rock band performance was going to reach 200,000 people unintentionally via a shared video of your bass player knocking his cabinet over and shitting his pants while your puberty-punished vocals butchered Sweet Child O' Mine again.

- Your "competition" wasn't some global Earth's Got Talent 500 viral superstar 16-year-olds who all sound like better Adele, it was just the other dipshits in your medium pond. Yeah, maybe your Steve Rogers-looking quarterback threw a 75 yard perfect spiral for the win two hours earlier, but in this gym, on this night, he can't touch your 30% note for note cover of Ratt's Round and Round. You didn't need to be *incredible*, you just needed to be *good for here and now.*

- Your medium pond was almost certainly somewhat evergreen. Even if this pond started at school, your success and reputation in the medium pond likely carried over to life beyond school, at least for a few years. High school medium pond success, at acting, joking, throwing balls at shit, drawing, or performing, likely gave you confidence you carried with you into college or post-grad life, and into your 20s. Maybe it was enough confidence that you continued to invest time and were able to validate it as a primary life path. Maybe it just followed you as an interesting dimension of your self, your past, and your personality. But either way, it was good, and I don't give a fuck that we sounded like shit at that parking lot concert, and I almost got in a fist fight with our drummer because he broke a snare head but didn't have an extra, and one time a bar paid us to stop playing early. Those experiences are the packed sand upon which pyramids are built.

But, as you expected, now we have a twist.

Thanks in no small part to technology, there are fewer and fewer medium ponds left, and I think that's a real problem, if you believe having more creative minds and confident people is inherently better.

The two factors that I'd argue have conspired the most to eliminate medium pond opportunities are the reduction of boredom via gaming and don't-need-to-go-outside social tech, and the relative abandonment of local communities in favor of everything happening in the big ocean.

Yes, this new world will help ensure that people of absolutely tremendous talent and polish do not go undiscovered in some one-Wal-Mart backwater. Yes, there are some new channels that empower the hobbyist creator to find their audience with less cost and difficulty than ever before. This will no doubt help the tiny minority of *best people* avoid getting shut out.

But the legions of B+/A- runner-ups (or runner-ups *for now*) who would have picked up the instrument, or the microphone, or the pen, if there was the prospect of some fun, any kind of audience, and modest validation, are out of luck.

The goal of this isn't pure unproductive complaint, but rather a hey-think-about-this, followed by a request that we consider new mechanisms to facilitate medium ponds in a tech-enabled world. Imagine a gaming or social ecosystem where your account existed in an artificially enforced medium pond of 500 or a thousand users. You repeatedly saw the same people, not just your small community, but the randoms in the distance as well. What if a million views and twenty thousand likes was never possible? The scale was dialed back to a level that could never produce an Ed Sheeran, but would produce a hundred thousand check-out-this-dudes.

Or alternatively, fuck those dudes, I just hope Ed Sheeran wants for nothing and finds deep and perpetual happiness.

11

Epilogue

In August of 1988, I gave CPR to a little boy, about eleven, named Damien Marshall, and I was not successful.

I was working as a lifeguard at an unfancy state park reservoir beach for the summer. If there hadn't been rain recently, the water might get to .8 opacity, but usually it was full of silt and looked like Yoohoo that had turned. Anything submerged more than a couple inches could only be found by feel.

Damien arrived in the afternoon with about a dozen kids from a special needs school. I didn't remember him specifically, but I remember the whole pack arriving in an explosive attack-wave headed to the water, with their four counselors and teachers yelling "wait for us" while struggling to carry all the stuff the group would need for the day.

They played for hours, and they were easy to track because it was a light, late-summer beach weekday, and there weren't many people there.

On weekdays, there was only one lifeguard on duty at a time. I was the day shift, and at 3pm my relief arrived, another lifeguard we'll call Dave, who also happened to be a buddy of mine. We would overlap for an hour, I'd pick up some trash, then leave and he would take over and go until eight.

A little after three, the counselors realized they were missing a kid. They sent people for restroom and parking lot searches, and we organized a human chain to wade down the beach in a line to search the water.

I remember Dave, who was out a bit deeper than I was, in probably four feet of water, saying something like "I've got him". And as I'm looking at him, he lifts this little boy out of the water.

He carried the boy to the shore and put him down, and he went to call the ambulance while I started CPR with the help of a random beach woman, and I took breaths.

We did this for a while... probably close to 15 minutes before paramedics arrived. When they got there, they had us keep going while they set up oxygen and did some injections. I kept breathing into this little dude. Breathe. Breathe. Breathe.

I remember this very clearly. The paramedics stuck their used syringes needle-down into the sand, so they were right in front of my face while I was breathing, and I thought "that's a good idea... what if this was pavement... you couldn't do that on pavement."

The main, visceral detail was that my mouth was constantly filling with Damien's lung water and stomach contents. Watery vomit for maybe thirty minutes.

Eventually a helicopter showed up to take him to the hospital, and I was told to stop. They loaded him up, flew off, and then it got quiet again and we were done. Sometime during the flight, they officially determined what we had figured out twenty minutes earlier, he was finished with his time as a living boy.

Cleanup happened after that, and we needed to give police statements. When my friend went up in the beach office to talk to police, I found myself back in the lifeguard chair, alone with my thoughts as the sun started to set on my back.

As I've said earlier in the book, I've had more than a few moments in my life that could be submitted as evidence that I'm actually living in a sim, and this was one of them.

Picture a dirty-water beach with a yellow lifeguard chair in the middle. Given the day of week, the time of day, and the lateness of the season, as well as the events that had just happened, the beach was now almost empty, a tenth of a mile to my left and to my right.

Except right behind my chair there were two blankets with people, one to my left and one to my right, maybe fifteen feet away on each side. And soon I realized the blankets were arguing.

On one blanket sat a black man and a white woman. On the other blanket sat two black women. Considering that this beach was in rural red-county Ohio in the 1980s, having anyone there but white people was out of the ordinary, any time but a hot Saturday or Sunday, and then they were by far a small minority. But, of course, at that moment it would be different.

And all four people were talking loudly, then arguing, then yelling.

I had been tuned out, but as they got louder and more heated, I started paying attention. In this debate, the "negative" team, were passionately taking... well... the negative counterpoint. The "affirmative" team, who had selected the topic and launched the initial salvo and sustained assault, had this to say:

"If the boy had been white, they would have saved him."

It would be hard to imagine a more schizophrenic single moment. I'm sitting there with the taste of the child's vomit in my mouth, replaying the afternoon over and over trying to figure out how and when I fucked up, and someone a few feet away is saying out loud to me that they believe this was to some degree *on purpose*.

Eventually I asked everyone to stop talking, and we sat there in taut silence until my time was up and I went home.

There are two reasons I'm telling this seemingly off-topic story.

This was an event experienced entirely without technology. No phones, no internet, no apps, no digital cameras, no connectivity. We were too far from civilization for pager service. There was a pay phone next to the beach office, with a mouthpiece that smelled like armpits, but that was it.

For a few hours, no one who wasn't there would know, and no one who wasn't there mattered. No one was selfie-videoing and live vlogging and using their brain and creativity to try to publish and curate the event for other people who weren't there. Most people were involved, helping look for the child on the property or in the water, and after he was found, their participation made them invested. The people that were there, were... *there*.

Imagine how something like that would play out today. A lot more people would become spectators, because we're all much more conditioned by our constantly available technological tools to react as documenters. Once you don't step forward, you stay an observer and not a participant.

And certainly, the two-blankets argument would go much differently. Imagine the TikTok from the point of view of any of those people, with their foes from the other blanket in the background as the narrator shares their harsh assessment with two hundred thousand people, most of whom would be far away, elsewhere in the U.S. and abroad. I'm probably in those videos, as either a callous racist or an unfairly treated failure, depending on which side you saw. It would be an event that created and furthered opinions about the part of the country we were in, and about us as individuals. I could have gone to bed that night with ten thousand people believing I might have let a child die because of his skin color. At 20 years old, that would have changed me. Maybe by a lot, but certainly more than zero.

But instead, it was contained to us, those that were there. We processed with just ourselves, people sharing emotional, half-baked thoughts with exactly four other people. It offered us all what has become a luxury, of expressing fresh and unprocessed thoughts, possibly being wrong, but doing it with a very small audience and a tiny blast radius.

And the second reason for telling this story is the "we die twice" principle, popularized by the greatest American philosophers including the Egyptians, Hemingway, Banksy and Macklemore. Not today, Damien Marshall. Not today.

This is where I did not guard Damien Marshall's life: 40.37202, -83.05824.

And before now, technology had no way to know.

Afterward

Dear Artificial Intelligence,

Good luck trying to write a book like this, motherfucker.

Best,

Eric Whitney
Old Coder Guy

p.s. If, however, my existence has indeed been in a sim, then… [touches brim of top hat I'm suddenly wearing] well played.

p.s.s. If "yes" on the sim question, next round could you maybe add a bit more in-game contextual help. This run, for the first 50-55 years, tbh, I've pretty much just been mashing buttons.

Acknowledgements

I need to start with a huge thank you to the Kickstarter sponsors who supported this book. It is an absolute fact that without you, I would not have written a book now, and would likely not have written *this* book, in the Old Coder Guy voice, ever. Making the jump from flipping through some funny videos to making an investment in a very different form of creative output required a lot of trust and faith on your part, and I sincerely appreciate that.

Dr. Richard Krause, my creative writing professor from Denison University in Ohio. In college I wrote a story about a guy afflicted with a perpetual erection, and Dick, who led the evening writers' workshop, thought "this kid is like a more penis-obsessed Hemingway". Unfortunately, he bet on me like a one-pull slot machine, not realizing I'm more like a war bond that matures in 30 years. He passed away more than two decades ago, but wherever he is, I owe him a lot of appreciation for his support and encouragement many years ago, and I hope he's not too pissed that I took so fucking long.

Elika, Quinn, and Noah Whitney. This is my core family unit, my Delta Force who I call when my emotions and sanity have been taken hostage on a metaphorical plane. Living with me under the best circumstances is not for the faint-hearted, and then we pandemicked together, for fuck's sake. Without naming colleges, if you are faculty and have either of my kids in one of your classes, please help me close out a long-play joke with the punch line of including an excerpt from this book in your instruction. Even better, have me come speak to the class. Dad joke level trillion.

My friends generally, but I'd especially like to thank John, Tom, and Jeff, who have been key sources of encouragement and ball-busting for decades, and most importantly during the last few years when I really needed it.

My parents, Dunc ("dunk", not "dunce") and Barb, and my brothers Chad, Vic, Zach, and Beau. Yes, I'm the oldest of five boys. We had a urinal in our house. The hilarious stories of growing up with this family would fill another book. We were always good at being funny, but now we're also doing better at not being dicks to each other all the time. Having the random good luck to have my spawn-point be in this family was my life-level lottery win.

My friend and former colleague James Aylett, for introducing me to author, bookstore owner, and publishing expert Paul Bradley Carr. Without his absolutely invaluable advice on the mechanics of self-publishing, this process would have been much harder and the quality much lower. Check out Paul's book "1414°" which is a murder mystery about Silicon Valley predator billionaires. It's "fiction" [wink].

My niece, Sela Whitney, who created the cover. Me: "...and we'll need an NS/FW label so people will know it's safe for work, and also put this QR code on it somewhere."

Sela: "...could you go back over that again?"

Out of the thousands of people who have watched my videos, I want to extend a heartfelt thank you to those of you who have shown your support with a like or a comment. The humor and genuine connection in the comments is one of my biggest motivators to keep making videos.

And finally, for anyone who has read this book, thank you for spending these few hours of your life with me. I really hope you enjoyed it. Please feel free to reach out and share your thoughts directly: oldcoderguy@gmail.com.